A GRAMMAR —FOR— BIBLICAL HEBREW

HANDBOOK

D1430922

A GRAMMAR —FOR— BIBLICAL HEBREW
HANDBOOK
ANSWER KEYS AND STUDY GUIDE

JEFFRIES M. HAMILTON
AND
JEFFREY S. ROGERS

ABINGDON PRESS
Nashville

ABINGDON PRESS
Nashville

A Grammar for Biblical Hebrew Handbook

This book is printed on acid-free paper.

ISBN 0-687-15685-8

Manufactured by the Parthenon Press at
Nashville, Tennessee, United States of America

INTRODUCTION

This volume was begun at the suggestion of Prof. C. L. Seow. As a companion to his <u>A Grammar for Biblical Hebrew</u>, it is intended to assist students in the mastery of basic elements of the language.

Two groups of students in particular should find it helpful.

For many, it is difficult to bridge the gap between the lively, supportive arena of the classroom and the lonely one-on-one confrontation with the <u>Grammar</u> when it is time to master the lesson and do the exercises. We have found that restatements of the lessons such as we have undertaken here are helpful at this point.

A second group is made up of those who find it necessary to study Hebrew on their own either for the first time or for review. The <u>Handbook</u> points these students to essential aspects of the <u>Grammar</u>, so that they get a sense of relative importance among the many parts of each lesson.

Each lesson here corresponds to the lesson of the same number in the <u>Grammar</u> and usually contains five sections:

Take Special Note calls attention to particularly important or difficult aspects of the lesson.

Review the Lesson reviews the basics.

Check Your Exercises supplies an answer key to the exercises at the end of each lesson, so that students receive immediate feedback to their work. When confronted with a discrepancy, most students are able to search the <u>Grammar</u> successfully for the reason for the discrepancy, and thus learning is enhanced by their referring to the key. Class time may then be spent where genuine problems exist rather than with momentary confusions which students could have corrected on their own. Beginning with Lesson 13, translations are no longer provided, as students may easily

refer to a standard translation. Instead, aspects
of the Hebrew text are highlighted, with direction
to appropriate parts of the <u>Grammar</u> for review.

You Should Know reminds students of the essentials of the lesson. These essentials are merely
listed; it is hoped that this list will then serve
as a checklist for exam review.

Did You Get It? offers a few additional drills
on material in the exercises.

In addition, four **Practical Helps** have been
included to give instruction in areas of particular
difficulty.

We are indebted to Prof. Seow for his encourage-
ment and criticism; to Prof. James F. Armstrong
who, along with Prof. Seow, allowed earlier versions
of the study guide to be tested in his classes;
to the many students and friends who offered their
assistance and criticism; to Princeton Theological
Seminary for the use of the Ibycus computer; to
Furman University for its support; to the editors
at Abingdon Press who have been supportive and
accommodating; and to our wives, Sarah and Bev,
who have been patient with us throughout the process.
The shortcomings of the project are, of course,
our own.

J. M. H.
J. S. R.

TABLE OF CONTENTS

LESSON 1

Take Special Note

1. The alphabet (́alep̄-bêt̲!) must be committed to
   memory <u>as quickly as possible</u>. Practice
   writing each letter until you can do so with
   confidence. Practice writing the entire
   alphabet in order. Remember, Hebrew reads from
   right to left, so practice writing that way,
   too!

2. A number of letters may look alike to you at
   first. Notice the differences.

   a. **bêt̲**

      כ/ב Bêt̲'s base extends to the right; kap̄'s
      does not.

   b. **dā́let̲**

      ר/ד Dā́let̲ is squared, but **rêš** is rounded.

      ך/ד Dā́let̲ stands on the line; final **kap̄**
      reaches below it.

   c. **hē**

      ח/ה Hē is open; **ḥēt̲** is closed (as is the
      throat as you pronounce them).

   d. **wāw**

      ז/ו Wāw has a small head; **zá́yin** wears
      a mortarboard.

      י/ו Wāw stands on the line, but **yōd̲** hangs
      in mid air.

   e. **zá́yin** (ז/ו, see d. above)

   f. **ḥēt̲** (ח/ה, see c. above)

      ת/ח The left leg of **ḥēt̲** lacks the small
      foot of **tāw**.

   g. **yōd̲** (י/ו, see d. above)

   h. **kap̄** (כ/ב, see a. above; ך/ד, see b. above)

      נ/כ Kap̄ has a large head and foot; **nûn** has
      small ones.

      ן/ך Final **kap̄** has a large head, but final
      nûn's is small.

      ר/ך Final **kap̄** is squared and reaches
      below the line; **rêš** is rounded and
      stands on the line.

   i. **mêm**

      ס/ם Final **mêm** is squared at the lower
      right hand corner, but **sāmek̲** is rounded

1

Lesson 1

(and final **mêm** can <u>only</u> occur in final position in a word!).

j. **nûn** (נ/כ, ן/ך, see h. above)
k. **sāmek** (ס/ם, see i. above)
l. **`áyin**
   ע/ץ The fork of `áyin is lower than the fork of **ṣādē**.
m. **ṣādē** (ץ/ע, see l. above)
n. **rêš** (ר/ד, see b. above; ר/ך, see h. above)
o. **śîn/šîn**
   שׂ/שׁ It's all in the dot: left **śîn**, right **šîn**.
p. **tāw** (ת/ח, see f. above)
q. Because the differentiation of the sounds represented is not familiar to speakers of non-Semitic languages, some letters may give you trouble in pronunciation and vocabulary words. Watch out for א/ע, ח/כ, ט/ת, כ/ק, and ס/שׂ.

Review the Lesson

1. Five letters take a different form at the end of a word (I.2.c, p. 3). Four unroll and drop an anchor; the fifth becomes a block:
   כ - ך   נ - ן   פ - ף   צ - ץ   מ - ם

2. Four letters are gutturals, and five cannot be doubled: א, ה, ח, and ע (the gutturals) and ר cannot be doubled (I.3, p. 3).

3. A **dāḡēš** is a dot in a consonant (I.5, p. 5).
   a. Gutturals and ר are off limits to the **dāḡēš**.
   b. A **dāḡēš** makes a **bĕḡad kĕpat** letter (בגד כפת) a stop, and sometimes doubles it, too.
   c. The other consonants are simply doubled. "A **dāḡēš-dot** means doubling; a **dāḡēš-dot** means stop:" **Dāḡēš forte** = doubling; **dāḡēš lene** = stop.

Lesson 1

Check Your Exercises

A.

1.	ישראל	8.	ציץ	15.	סום
2.	הלך	9.	מלך	16.	מעט
3.	צלמות	10.	חשך	17.	כנען
4.	יונתן	11.	שרים	18.	קיריה
5.	טוב	12.	באר	19.	כפים
6.	הערים	13.	יעופף	20.	כמוהו
7.	גנב	14.	זרוע		

B.
(1) brˊšyt̠ brˊ ˊlhym ˊt̠ hššmym wˊt̠ hˊrṣ (2) whˊrṣ
hyt̠h t̠hw wb̠hw whšk̠ ˋl pny t̠hwm wrwḥ ˊlhym mrḥp̠t̠ ˋl
pny hmmym (3) wyyˊmr ˊlhym yhy ˊwr wyhy ˊwr
(4) wyyrˊ ˊlhym ˊt̠ hˊwr ky t̠wb̠ wyyb̠dl ˊlhym byn
hˊwr wb̠yn hḥšk̠

You Should Know

1. The letters of the Hebrew alphabet in order.
2. How to transliterate Hebrew letters into their
   English equivalents and vice versa.
3. The gutturals and the behavior which distin-
   guishes them from the other letters.
4. What a **dāḡēš** does.

Did You Get It?

1. Write the alphabet in order (from right to
   left!)
2. Write the five letters which take final forms.
   Write the final forms.
3. Write the four gutturals and the five letters
   which cannot be doubled.
4. Write the **bĕḡad kĕp̄āt** letters with and without
   a **dāḡēš.**

(Check your answers by the appropriate sections of
the Handbook or the Grammar.)

3

Take Special Note

1. **The Hebrew vowels**, their names, classes, and lengths must be commited to memory <u>as soon as possible</u>. Practice writing and naming each vowel according to its classification (**a, i, u**).

2. Your <u>Grammar</u> classifies the vowels into three groups: **a, i,** and **u** (II.1, p. 7). This is a phonetic classification. Thus, **a** = ä as in "cär," **i** = ē as in "ēven," and **u** = o͞o as in "to͞ol." <u>Do not let this terminology confuse you</u>. Learn the Hebrew vowels according to the three phonetic classifications, **a, i, u**.

3. The various ways of denoting vowel sounds in Hebrew are given in your <u>Grammar</u> in the charts on pp. 7, 9, and 11. The following chart assembles all these forms according to their phonetic classifications.

a	i	u
ָ הָ	ִ ◌ֹ ◌ֹ ה ִ	◌ֹ וֹ הֹ
ְ	◌ֹ ◌ֹ ◌ֹ ◌ֹ ה	◌ֹ ◌ֹ ◌ֹ ◌ֹ וּ
◌ֹ ◌ֹ	◌ֹ ◌ֹ ◌ֹ ◌ֹ ה	◌ֹ
◌ֹ	◌ֹ	◌ֹ

Notice that the vowels written as **matres lectionis** are different ways of writing the same sound. The **matres** represent a distinction in the writing system, <u>not</u> in pronunciation.

4. To help you with Exercise 2.B (p. 14) **Practical Help 1** following this lesson presents a step-by-step guide to dividing Hebrew words into syllables. You must master this basic exercise as soon as possible.

Lesson 2

Review the Lesson

1. **Simple vowels.**
   a. Length (II.1, pp. 7-8).

a		i		u	
long	short	long	short	long	short
ָ	ַ	ִ	ִ		ֻ
		long/short		long/short	
		ִ			ֻ

   b. Two vowels aren't always what they seem to be:
   - i. ָ may be either long **a** (**qāmēṣ**) or short **o** (**qāmēṣ ḥāṭûp̄**)--review II.8, pp. 12-13;
   - ii. ַ may be a furtive ("sneaky") **páṯaḥ**-- review II.9, p. 13.

2. **Matres Lectionis** (II.2, pp. 8-10).
   a. Three consonants aren't always what they seem to be: ה, ׳, and ו may indicate long vowels. Note the **matres**, the vowel classes, and the vowels with which each is associated.

	a	i		u
ה	הָ	הִ	הִ	הֹ
׳		׳	׳	׳
ו				וֹ וּ

   b. **Definitions** (II.3, p. 10):
   - i. A vowel written with a **mater** is said to be "full."
   - ii. A vowel written without a **mater** (though it could employ one) is said to be "defective."
   c. ה at the end of a word could be either a **mater** or a real consonant. When it is a real consonant it is marked with a dot called a **mappîq** (הּ) (II.2.h, p. 9).

5

Lesson 2

3. šĕwā´.
   a. Simple šĕwā´ may be either vocal or silent
      (II.4, pp. 10-11).

vocal	silent
(a) beginning of word	(a) end of word
(b) second of two together	(b) first of two
(c) after doubled consonant	(c) after stressed vowel
(d) after unaccented long vowel	(d) after unaccented short vowel

   b. There are three composite šĕwā´'s, one for
      each vowel class (II.5, p. 11):

a	i	u
־ֲ	־ֱ	־ֳ

   Remember, gutturals take composite šĕwā´ in
   place of simple vocal šĕwā´.

4. **Stress or Accent** (II.6, pp. 11-12).
   a. The stress usually falls on the last
      syllable (the ultima), less frequently on
      the next to last (penultima). Notice that
      the terms ultima and penultima refer to
      the position of the syllable in a word
      regardless of where the stress falls.
   b. The stressed syllable is called the "tonic"
      syllable, the syllable before it is the
      "pretonic," and the syllable before that
      the "propretonic." Notice that the
      positions of the syllables referred to by
      these terms will change depending on where
      the stress falls.
   c. Observe מְלָכִים and יִשְׁמְרֵהוּ :

```
ult|pen|              ult|pen|   |
כִים |לָ |מְ          הוּ|רֵ | מְ |יִשׁ
ton|pre|pro           |ton|pre|pro
```

5. To review **syllables** in Hebrew words (II.7, pp.
   12-13), see **Practical Help 1**.

6. Three consonants aren't always what they seem
   to be, and four are not pronounced. Three are
   the **matres**, ה, ‘, and ו, which indicate long
   vowels; the fourth is the quiescent א, which
   is not pronounced even though it is written in
   the text (II.10, p. 13).

Check Your Exercises

A. and B.

1. יַעֲ|קֹב	6. רְ|אוּ|בֵן	11. וַיְ|הִי
2. חָכְ|מָה	7. וִי|הוּ|דָה	12. אִשָּׁה (אִשׁ|שָׁה)
3. שָׁ|מוֹת	8. אַ|רוֹן	13. אִישׁ
4. לֵ|וִי	9. סוּ|סוֹ	14. מַלְ|אָ|כִי
5. גָּ|בוֹהַּ	10. שָׂ|דֶה	15. שֹׁ|מֵעַ

C.

1.	ʾădāmā(h)	ground	9.	hṓdeš	month
2.	hādāš	new	10.	qṓdeš	holiness
3.	bĕrît	covenant	11.	dābār	word
4.	ʿôlām	forever	12.	qôl	voice
5.	šáʿar	gate	13.	zāhāb	gold
6.	késep	silver	14.	gôy	nation
7.	nābî(ʾ)	prophet	15.	ʾôr	light
8.	kōhēn	priest			

You Should Know

1. The vowel sounds, their names, classes, and
   lengths.
2. The **matres lectionis**.
3. The **mappîq**.
4. Simple and composite **šĕwāʾ**.
5. The occurrence of stress in a word.
6. The division of words into syllables.
7. The distinction between **qāmēṣ** and **qāmēṣ ḥāṭûp**.
8. Furtive **pátaḥ**.
9. Quiescent א.

Did You Get It?

Write the following in Hebrew and divide into syllables.

1. ´ōhel
2. `ābād
3. ´ādām

4. kōhēn
5. mélek
6. `ébed

(Check yourself by the vocabulary list in Lesson II in your <u>Grammar</u> and the acceptable patterns for syllables given in **Practical Help 1**, section 2.e, in your <u>Handbook</u>.)

PRACTICAL HELP 1: BEGINNING
SYLLABLE DIVISION

1. Dividing Hebrew words into syllables becomes
   second nature with practice. At first, it's a
   matter of trial and error. Use the procedures
   below to speed you to correct division.

2. Syllable division is accomplished by applying
   the following rules and patterns for syllables. A syllable:
   a. always begins with a consonant (C),
   b. has only one vowel (v = short vowel,
      v̄ = long vowel, v̆ = vocal **šĕwāʼ**, or
      v̂ = vowel written with a **mater**),
   c. may be open (ending in a vowel--Cv́, Cv̄, Cv̆,
      or Cv̂) or closed (ending in a consonant
      CvC or Cv́C),
   d. may be accented or unaccented:
      i. a long vowel in a closed syllable <u>must</u>
         be accented (Cv́C);
      ii. a short vowel in an open syllable <u>must</u>
          be accented (Cv́);
      iii. thus the patterns Cv̄C unaccented and Cv
           unaccented are <u>not</u> acceptable.
   e. Thus, <u>the acceptable patterns</u> are Cv́, Cv̄,
      Cv̆, Cv̂, CvC, or Cv̆C.
   (Remember that furtive **pátaḥ** does not count as
   a vowel.)

3. Step-by-step division (It pays to use Hebrew
   rather than transliteration!)
   EXAMPLE A: וִיהוּדָה

   a. <u>Always work back</u> from the end of the word
      to the beginning.
      ----->
      וִיהוּדָה

   b. Working back, go to the first vowel (ָ)
      and the consonant preceding (ד). Divide
      at that point.
      וִיהוּ|דָה

      Check to see that your division produces
      an acceptable pattern (see 2.e above). Cv̂
      is allowed, so move on.

c. Work back to the next vowel (וּ) and the
    consonant preceding (ה). Divide at that
    point.

    וְ|יִ|הוּ|דָה

    Check your division, and you see that that
    pattern Cv̂ is allowed. Move on.
d. Work back to the next vowel (יִ) and the
    consonant preceding (י).

    וְ|יִ|הוּ|דָה

    Check your division to see that the pattern
    Cv̂ is acceptable (it is, of course). Since
    you are at the beginning of the word and
    have accounted for every syllable according
    to the acceptable patterns in 2 above, your
    work is done.

NOTE HOW STEP-BY-STEP DIVISION WORKS:
    Work Back
    First Vowel, Consonant Preceding
    Divide
    Check
Practice this procedure with the next example.
EXAMPLE B: מַלְאָכִי

a. Working back (--->), take the first vowel
    (כִ) and the consonant preceding (כ).
    Divide.

    מַלְאָ|כִי

    The pattern Cv̂ is acceptable. Move on.
b. Take the next vowel (אָ) and the consonant
    preceding (א). Divide.

    מַלְ|אָ|כִי

    Cv̄ is allowed. Move on.
c. Take the next vowel (לְ) and the consonant
    preceding (ל). <u>Whenever</u> the next vowel is
    a **šĕwā´**, you must be on your toes. For
    now, go ahead and divide.

    מַ|לְ|אָ|כִי

    According to 2.e above Cv̄ is acceptable.
    However, notice what is left for the next
    syllable: מַ--Cv unaccented! <u>Cv unaccented
    is not acceptable</u>, so you must try another

10

division. Right now לְ is divided as if the
šĕwā´ were vocal (i.e., the next vowel).
Let's divide it as if it were silent (i.e.,
not a vowel at all). Take the first vowel
(ַ) and the consonant preceding (מ).
Divide.

מַלְ|אָ|כִי

Now the result is CvC, an acceptable pattern. Remember, whenever the next vowel
is a šĕwā´ you must be on your toes. It
will be either vocal (it counts as a
vowel) or silent (it does not count). You
will be able to decide which it is by
glancing at the pattern produced in the
next syllable.

The following example shows you both of these
šĕwā´'s at work.
EXAMPLE C: יִשְׁמְרוּ

a. Work back to the first vowel (וּ) and the
    consonant preceding (ר). Divide.

    יִשְׁמְ|רוּ

    Check Cv̆, move on.
b. Next vowel (ְ), consonant preceding (מ),
    divide.

    יִשְׁ|מְ|רוּ

    You know from the example above that Cv̆
    is allowed, but might not be correct.
    Glance at the syllable preceding: יִשְׁ.
    CvC is allowed, and since you have reached
    the beginning of the word, your work is
    done.

Notice how the šĕwā´'s work in the next one.
EXAMPLE D: דִּבְּרוּ

a. Work back to first vowel (וּ), consonant
    preceding (ר); divide.

    דִּבְּ|רוּ

    Check Cv̆, move on.
b. Next vowel (ְ), consonant preceding (בּ).
    Divide. But wait. Notice the dāḡēš in

11

the בּ. Since the בּ is preceded by a vowel
(ָ), the dages must meaning doubling. When
šěwā´ occurs under a doubled consonant,
shorthand is being used--what you really
have is two בּ's and two ְ 's: בְּבַ. To
represent this in syllable dividing, you
may draw your line through the **dāḡēš** in
the letter or by writing the letter
twice, as below.

דְּבְ|בְ|ר ֹ

Cv̆ is allowed, but since you are dealing
with a **šěwā´**, check the syllable preceding.
Since CvC is allowed and you have come to
the beginning of the word, your work is
done.

4. Occasionally you will be confronted by a word
or a syllable which will stump you at first.
As you follow the step-by-step procedure,
"Work Back, First Vowel and Consonant
Preceding, Divide, Check," play with the rules
and the patterns for syllables given in 2.
above. Eventually you will arrive at an
acceptable set of patterns, and you will have
divided the word properly.

    Where most people run into trouble is with
šěwā´'s and doubled consonants, so be especially alert when you come across them.

5. Note on Exercise 2.B.1: Syllable division
of יַעֲקֹב. All options for dividing this word
(יַ|עֲ|קֹב ; יַ|עֲקֹב ; and יַעֲ|קֹב) violate at
least one of the "rules" set forth in 2. above.
We have preferred יַעֲ|קֹב--remember that Cv
unaccented is unacceptable!

Take Special Note

1. **Endings.** The most important new concept found in this lesson is that of endings. Endings will occur on nouns, verbs, adjectives and prepositions. It is extremely important that you learn to spot endings and let them help you recognize the form of the word in question. Whenever new endings are presented, make a special effort to learn them as quickly and as thoroughly as possible. Extra effort at the outset will save you much grief later.

2. **Vowel reduction** (or What to Do When You Stick Something on the End).
   a. Add the ending (plural, dual, fs).
      i. Be sure to change final forms to medial:
      ;עוֹלָמִים <-- עוֹלָם
      ii. Be sure to remove final ה ָ :
      רֵעָה [fs] <-- רֵעֶה [ms].
   b. Count back two vowels (not counting the ending you just added), and reduce that vowel if you can (see c. below).
      i. ָ and ֵ in an open syllable go to šĕwāʹ:
      דְּבָרִים <-- *דְּבָרִים <-- דָּבָר + mp ending
      לְבָבוֹת <-- *לֵבָבוֹת <-- לֵבָב + fp ending
      ii. Beneath a guttural, use composite šĕwāʹ:
      חֲכָמָה <-- *חָכָמָה <-- חָכָם + fs ending
      עֲנָבִים <-- *עֵנָבִים <-- עֵנָב + mp ending
   c. Vowels that cannot be reduced:
      i. long vowels written with a **mater**:
      הֵיכָלִים <-- הֵיכָל + mp ending
      ii. long **o**:
      כֹּהֲנִים <-- כֹּהֵן + mp ending
      iii. any vowel in a closed syllable:
      מִלְחָמוֹת <-- מִלְחָמָה + fp ending
   d. If you cannot reduce that vowel, try the one to its left: ֵ in an open syllable

13

Lesson 3

may be reduced (but not ָ).

מוֹעֲדִים <-- ‎*מוֹעֲדִים <-- מוֹעֵד‎ + mp ending

כּוֹכָבִים <-- כּוֹכָבִים <-- כּוֹכָב‎ + mp ending

   e. In words with contractible vowel clusters (or dipthongs):

מָוֶת --> מוֹתִים   זַיִת --> זֵיתִים

(You must simply memorize these patterns.)

Review the Lesson

1. Gender and number are marked by endings (III.1, pp. 15-17).
    a. masculine singular (ms): no special ending
    b. masculine plural (mp): ‎ ‍ים‎ -
    c. feminine singular (fs): ‎ה‎ָ - or ‎ת‎- (but sometimes no ending)
    d. feminine plural (fp): ‎וֹת‎- ,
    e. dual (for both m and f): ‎ַיִם‎-

Check Your Exercises

A.

1. בָּמוֹת	11. מִלְחָמוֹת	21. כּוֹכָבִים
2. שִׁירִים	12. חֲכָמִים	22. הֵיכָלִים
3. אֲדוֹנִים	13. צְדָקוֹת	23. בְּהֵמוֹת
4. צַדִּיקִים	14. דְּבָרִים	24. לְבָבוֹת
5. יָדוֹת	15. גִּבּוֹרִים	25. מִשְׁפָּחוֹת
6. אֵלִים	16. מַלְאָכִים	26. כֹּהֲנִים
7. אֵילִים	17. זְקֵנִים/-וֹת	27. יְשׁוּעוֹת
8. עוֹלָמִים	18. מְנָחוֹת	28. תּוֹרוֹת
9. אַמּוֹת	19. עוֹלוֹת	29. עֲנָבִים
10. מוֹעֲדִים	20. חוֹמוֹת	30. דָּמִים

B.

1. פָּנִים	5. נְבִיאִים	9. מַיִם
2. יָדַיִם	6. שָׁמַיִם	10. עֵינַיִם
3. אֵל/אֱלֹהִים	7. כֹּהֲנִים	11. מִשְׁפָּטִים
4. אָזְנַיִם	8. אַמּוֹת	12. אֲדָמָה

14

You Should Know

1. The noun endings--masculine and feminine; singular, dual, and plural.
2. The vowel changes which occur when endings are added.

Did You Get It?

Give the plural of the following:

1. נָבִיא   5. שֹׁפֵט

2. חָכָם   6. זַ֫יִת

3. לֵבָב   7. מָ֫וֶת

4. עֵנָב   8. חֹזֶה

Give the dual of the following:

1. יָד   3. יוֹם

2. שָׁנָה

(Check yourself by sections III.3, pp. 18-19, and III.1.e, pp. 16-17, in the Grammar.)

Take Special Note

1. Because Hebrew words are usually comprised of
    three root letters, it is convenient to refer
    to patterns of word formation with letters or
    numbers which represent a given consonant in
    a particular position in a word. Two systems
    are used in your <u>Grammar</u> (IV.1, p. 21). The
    chart below shows how they correspond.

ק (**q**)	= first consonant in the root =	I
ט (**ṭ**)	= second consonant in the root =	II
ל (**l**)	= third consonant in the root =	III

2. Pay particular attention to discussions 4 and
    5 concerning geminate and segolate nouns in
    Review the Lesson below.

3. Be sure to learn the irregular plurals on p.
    28 in your <u>Grammar</u>, since they occur often.

4. To help you with Exercise 4.A (p. 30) **Practical
    Help 2** following this lesson presents tips
    for finding roots in nouns.

Review the Lesson

1. **Weak radicals** (IV.2, pp. 21-24).
    a. Gutturals (א, ה, ח, ע) and ר.
        i. Since gutturals and ר cannot be
            doubled, in place of doubling expect
            one of two things:
            α. compensatory lengthening of the
                vowel preceding the guttural

a	i	u
ָ to ַ	ִ to ֵ	ֻ to ׁ

            β. or virtual doubling (= no change
                in the preceding vowel).
        ii. Expect composite šĕwāʾ (ֱ, ֲ, ֳ) instead
             of simple šĕwāʾ under gutturals.
        iii. Gutturals prefer a-class vowels.

b. נ followed directly by a consonant is assimilated and the consonant is doubled ("the נ rolls up and becomes a **dāḡēš**"): מנקטל becomes מקטל. Remember, gutturals and ר are off limits to a **dāḡēš**, so expect compensatory lengthening or virtual doubling if the consonant after the נ is a guttural or ר.

c. ו and י .

   i. When is a I-י root not a I-י root? When it was originally I-ו.

   ii. When is a III-ה root not a III-ה root? When it was originally III-ו or III-י .

   iii. Remember, when ו and י occur in a contractible vowel cluster, מָוֶת --> מוֹתִים זָיִח --> זֵיתִים.

2. The three consonants which occur as prefixes on nouns are מ, ח, and א. They are not a part of the root (IV.3, pp. 24-26).

3. **Geminate nouns** (IV.4, pp. 26-27).

   a. These might cause you difficulty in the masculine singular, because the double final radical (think "gemini," twins) appears only once: עַם, "people," from the root עמם. You will not have trouble with the feminine singular and plurals, since the **dāḡēš** will show you the double radical: חֻקּוֹת, "statutes," from the root חקק.

   b. Two special cases.

      i. Remember, gutturals and ר are off limits to the **dāḡēš**, so expect compensatory lengthening: פַּר. "bull," but פָּרָה "cow," from the root פרר.

      ii. Remember, נ followed directly by a consonant "rolls up and becomes a **dāḡēš**" in the consonant: אַף, "nose," but אַפַּיִם, "noses," from the root אנף. (Notice that the few nouns of this type are not really from geminate roots but behave as though they were.)

17

4. Segolate nouns (think **sĕḡōl**, ˌ) are a small group who play by their own rules (IV.5, pp. 27-28).

   a. For the singular, use this working definition: a segolate is a two-syllable noun with the accent on the first syllable and a **sĕḡōl** (ˌ) or a "segol-substitute" (such as **páṯaḥ** (ˍ) because of a guttural) in at least one syllable.

      i. מֶ֫לֶךְ, "king"--two syllables, accent on the first, **sĕḡōl** in at least one syllable.

      ii. עֵ֫זֶר, "help"--two syllables, accent on the first, **sĕḡōl** in at least one.

      iii. אֹ֫הֶל, "tent"--two syllables, accent on the first, **sĕḡōl** in at least one.

      iv. זֶ֫רַע, "seed"--two syllables, accent on the first, **sĕḡōl** in at least one.

      v. נַ֫עַר, "lad"--two syllables, accent on the first, and a **sĕḡōl**-substitute (**páṯaḥ** because of the guttural-- remember, gutturals prefer **a**-class vowels).

   b. For the plural, <u>you must learn</u> the segolate plural pattern, which all segolates follow-- vocal **šĕwā´** under the first consonant, **qāmēṣ** under the second:

(f) קְטָלוֹת	(m) קְטָלִים
נֶ֫פֶשׁ --> נְפָשׁוֹת	מֶ֫לֶךְ --> מְלָכִים

      i. Remember, you expect composite **šĕwā´** under gutturals:
         אֶ֫רֶץ --> אֲרָצוֹת

      ii. Don't be surprised that when the original vowel of a segolate is **u**-class (e.g., אֹ֫הֶל, חֹ֫דֶשׁ), the **u**-class composite **šĕwā´** is used (e.g., אֳהָלִים, חֳדָשִׁים).

Lesson 4

Check Your Exercises

A.

1.	חעב	11.	שתה	21.	נור	31.	ענה
2.	בצר	12.	נוף	22.	חלל	32.	בטח
3.	נצב	13.	רעה	23.	יקש	33.	חשב
4.	נפל	14.	יצא	24.	קנה	34.	יצא
5.	זמר	15.	עשה	25.	נגף	35.	נסע
6.	יחן	16.	נבא	26.	אזן	36.	זרח
7.	חסה	17.	ילד	27.	ענה	37.	ראה
8.	לון	18.	חצה	28.	ירה	38.	לחם
9.	גור	19.	יתר	29.	נבט	39.	קדש
10.	קוה	20.	ילד	30.	כלה	40.	משל

B.

1.	מְלָכִים	11.	שָׂרִים	21.	הָרִים
2.	עֲבָדִים	12.	בָּנִים	22.	דְּרָכִים
3.	נְעָרִים	13.	בָּנוֹת	23.	אֹהָלִים
4.	נְפָשׁוֹת	14.	עַמִּים	24.	פָּרִים
5.	אֲרָצוֹת	15.	עָרִים	25.	אִמּוֹת
6.	עֲדָרִים	16.	בָּתִּים	26.	רָאשִׁים
7.	חֲדָשִׁים	17.	אֲנָשִׁים	27.	מַלְאָכִים
8.	חֻקִּים	18.	נָשִׁים	28.	אֲדוֹנִים
9.	יָמִים	19.	אָבוֹת	29.	כֵּלִים
10.	יַמִּים	20.	אַחִים	30.	מְקוֹמוֹת

You Should Know

1. How the paradigmatic root קטל (**qṭl**) is used in your grammar.
2. The weak radicals and their idiosyncrasies.
3. How to recognize nouns with prefixes.
4. Geminate nouns and segolate nouns.
5. The irregular plurals on p. 28 in your <u>Grammar</u>.

PRACTICAL HELP 2: ROOT—FINDING
IN NOUNS

The fastest way to find the root of a noun is to follow a process of elimination. If you are unsuccessful on the first or second try, don't panic. Although it is impossible to account for every noun, the steps outlined below will help you find most roots within three tries.

1. You are looking for three root letters.

2. Always work from the ends toward the middle, eliminating prefixes and suffixes.
   EXAMPLE A: מַחֲשָׁבָה
   i. הָ marks the fs--it is a suffix to be eliminated (III.1.b, p. 15).
      מַחֲשָׁב
   ii. מ (along with א and ת) is a common prefix--eliminate it (IV.3.a, p. 24).
      חשׁב is the root

3. Be alert for a **mater** in the noun (II.2.f, p. 9).
   EXAMPLE B: נְבִיאָה
   i. Eliminate the fs suffix.
      נְבִיא
   ii. You are left with four letters, but you recognize the ' of ' as a mater and eliminate it.
      נבא is the root.

4. Watch for a **dāḡēš forte**; it may mark a missing letter.
   EXAMPLE C: מַפֵּלֶח
   i. Eliminate the ת as a fs ending (III.1.b, p. 15).
      מַפֵּל
   ii. Eliminate the מ as a prefix (IV.3.a, p. 24).
      פֵּל
   iii. You are left with only two letters, but notice the **dāḡēš** in the first one. A נ has been assimilated (IV.2.b, p. 22) into the פ, so the root is נפל.

Practical Help 2

EXAMPLE D: תְּחִלָּה

  i.   Eliminate the fs ending (III.1.b, p. 15).
      תְּחִל

  ii. Eliminate the ת as a prefix (IV.3.b, p. 15).
      חִל

 iii. You are left with only two letters, but notice the **dāḡēš** in the second. There are really two ל's, so your root is חלל.

5. Sometimes you are left with two letters and no **dāḡēš** to guide you. In those cases you have three choices, one of which will be correct. The root is III-ה, II-ו/י, or geminate (think "gemini," twins).

EXAMPLE E: תִּקְוָה

  i.   Eliminate the fs ending (III.1.b., p. 15).
      תִּקְו

  ii. Eliminate the ת as a prefix (IV.3.b, p. 25).

      קְו

 iii. Your choices are קוה (III-ה), קוו or קיי (II-ו/י), and קוו (geminate); the first one is correct.

EXAMPLE F: מָגוֹר

  i.   Eliminate the מ as a prefix (IV.3.a, p. 24).

      גוֹר

  ii. Eliminate the ו as a **mater**.
      גר

 iii. Your choices are גרה (III-ה), גור (II-ו/י), and גרר (geminate); the second is correct.

EXAMPLE G: רָעָה

  i.   Eliminate the fs ending (III.1.b, p. 15).
      רָע

  ii. Your choices are רעה (III-ה), רוע (II-ו/י), and רעע (geminate). The third is correct.

Practical Help 2

6. If ו or י follows a prefix, you have two
   possibilities: I-ו/י (always listed in BDB as
   I-י) or the prefix is a root letter and the
   ו or י is a **mater**.
   EXAMPLE H: אֵיתָנִים

   i. Eliminate the mp ending (III.1.c, p. 16).
      אֵיתָן

   ii. You have two possibilities. The root is
       either יתן (I-ו/י) or אתן. The first is
       correct.

   EXAMPLE I: תּוֹעֵבָה

   i. Eliminate the fs ending (III.1.b, p. 15).
      תּוֹעֵב

   ii. You have two possibilities. The root is
       either יעב (I-ו/י) or תעב. The second is
       correct.

7. Miscellaneous cases:
   a. If a noun ends in הָ , it is III-ה (e.g.,
      מִקְנֶה is from קנה).
   b. If a noun ends in וֹן and you have no other
      clues, try III-נ, III-ה, or II-ו (e.g.,
      גָּאוֹן might be from גאן, גאה, or גוה; the
      second is correct).
   c. If a noun ends in ית or יִ , the root is
      probably III-ה (e.g., בְּרִית is from ברה).

8. If all else fails, try looking the noun up as
   it stands. For some particularly difficult
   cases, BDB will list the word and direct you to
   its root (e.g., עָתָּה is listed on p. 800, col.
   2, and you are directed to the root עוה).

22

LESSON 5

Review the Lesson

1. **The Definite Article** (V.1, pp. 31-32).

usual form	before ר,א	before ח,ה	before ע	before, חָ,חָ,עָ,הָ
הַ·	הָ	הַ	(הַ)הָ	הֶ

(Remember, gutturals and ר are off limits to the **dāḡēš**, so the form of the article changes. Before א and ר, compensatory lengthening occurs; before ה and ח, virtual doubling; and before ע, usually compensatory lengthening, but sometimes virtual doubling. The fourth group must simply be learned.)

2. **Prefixed Prepositions** בְּ, כְּ, and לְ (V.2, pp. 32-33).

usual form	rules of šĕwā´			with הַ·
	before ְ	before ְ	before ֲ ֳ ֱ	
בְּ	בִּ	בִּי	בָּ, בֶּ, בָּ	בַּ·
כְּ	כִּ	כִּי	כָּ, כֶּ, כָּ	כַּ·
לְ	לִ	לִי	לָ, לֶ, לָ	לַ·

a. Note that the preposition simply replaces the ה of the definite article and keeps the vowel of the article.
b. Two special cases.
   i. Before אֱלֹהִים: בֵּ, כֵּ, לֵ and the א quiesces (e.g., לֵאלֹהִים).
   ii. Before a stressed syllable, לְ is frequently לָ.

3. **Preposition מִן** (V.4, pp. 33-34).

unprefixed form	prefixed forms			
	usual form	before gutturals and ר	before ְ	before הַ·
מִן־	מִ·	(מֵ)מֵ	מִי	מִן־/מֵ

23

(Notice that the prefixed forms follow the rules for ‍נ‍ that you already know. In the usual form, ‍נ‍ assimilates. Before gutturals and ‍ר‍, compensatory lengthening or, rarely, virtual doubling occurs. Before ‍יְ‍, מִן acts like בְּ, כְּ, and לְ.)

4. **Conjunction** ‍ו‍ (V.5, pp. 34-35).

usual form	before פ, מ, ב	before ‍ְ‍	before ‍ְ‍	before ‍ֳ‍ ‍ֱ‍ ‍ֲ‍
וְ	וּ	וּ	וִי	וָ , וֶ , וַ

Two special cases.
  i. Before אֱלֹהִים: וֵ and the א quiesces (וֵאלֹהִים).
  ii. Before a stressed syllable, וְ is frequently וָ.

Check Your Exercises

A.
1. הָעָם	8. הַנָּשִׁים	15. הָאֲרָצוֹת
2. הַשָּׂרִים	9. הֶהָר	16. אֲרוֹן
3. הֶעָרִים	10. הַנְּבִיאִים	17. הָאָרוֹן
4. הָאִישׁ	11. הֶהָרִים	18. הַחֶרֶב
5. הָאָרֶץ	12. הַחַטָּאת	19. הַמְּלָכִים
6. הַהֵיכָל	13. הַחֹדֶשׁ	20. הַיַּמִּים
7. הֶעָוֹן	14. הָאֲנָשִׁים	

B.
1. בִּמְלָכִים	8. מֵהָרֹאשׁ	15. וּבֶעָרִים
2. לְעֶבֶד	9. בִּנְבִיאִים	16. לֵאלֹהִים
3. מֵהָאָרֶץ	10. כַּנְּבִיאִים	17. נָשִׁים וַאֲנָשִׁים
4. בַּהֵיכָל	11. הָאִישׁ וְהָאִשָּׁה	18. מִשָּׁמַיִם אֶל־אֶרֶץ
5. בְּחֶרֶב	12. מֵעִיר לָעִיר	19. מִיהוּדָה
6. בַּחֶרֶב	13. בָּאֲנָשִׁים	20. אָבוֹת וּבָנִים
7. בַּחֲרָבוֹת	14. בֶּהָרִים	

Lesson 5

C.
1. in place of David
2. silver and gold
3. before the ark
4. rulers and servants
5. to the presence of the Lord YHWH
6. between waters and waters
7. in front of the mountain
8. before Moses and Aaron
9. from day to night
10. with the festivals and new moons and sabbaths
11. for Judah
12. between God and living creature
13. face to face
14. the people and priest alike
15. after the king
16. after the darkness
17. the waters beneath the heavens
18. from before the priests
19. the waters in the seas
20. a hand in return for ("at the price of...") a hand, a foot in return for a foot

You Should Know

1. The forms of the definite article and the common words which are vocalized differently when they take the article.
2. The prefixed prepositions בְּ, כְּ, and לְ. How to prefix them to a word normally, when the word begins with šĕwāʾ, and when the word has the definite article.
3. The preposition מִן, in its form with **maqqēp** and in its prefixed forms.
4. The conjunction ו and how it is pointed.
5. The consonants which lose **dāḡēš forte** when followed by a šĕwāʾ (IV.6, p. 35).
6. The poetic, demonstrative, and vocative uses of the definite article (V.7, pp. 35-36).

25

LESSON 6

Take Special Note

The comparative use of the preposition מִן has
tripped up many a beginning student. Notice the
following examples.

חֲכָמָה הַמַּלְכָּה מֵהַמֶּֽלֶךְ

    The queen is wiser than the king.

קָטֹן דָּוִד מֵהָאַחִים

    David is smaller than the brothers.

When you see the preposition מִן, remember that it
could be the comparative (VI.3, p. 41).

Review the Lesson

1. **Inflection of Adjectives** (VI.1, pp. 39-40).
   You already know the inflectional endings of
   the adjective if you learned the endings of
   the noun in Lesson III. For the sake of
   review, here they are again:
   a. masculine singular (ms): no special ending
   b. masculine plural (mp): ־ ִים
   c. feminine singular (fs): ־ ָה
   d. feminine plural (fp): ־ וֹת
   e. No dual adjectives!

2. **Uses of the Adjective** (VI.2, pp. 40-41).

Attributive	Predicative	Substantive
אִשָּׁה טוֹבָה	טוֹבָה אִשָּׁה	—
"a good woman"	"a woman is good"	
הָאִשָּׁה הַטּוֹבָה	טוֹבָה הָאִשָּׁה	הַזָּקֵן
	הָאִשָּׁה טוֹבָה	
"the good woman"	"the woman is good"	"the old man/elder"

Notice that the construction אִשָּׁה טוֹבָה could
be either "a good woman" or "a woman is good."
You must decide from context which is correct.

26

Lesson 6

Check Your Exercises

A.

1.	אִישׁ צַדִּיק	8.	טוֹב הַדָּבָר	15.	בְּמָקוֹם קָדוֹשׁ
2.	גּוֹי קָדוֹשׁ	9.	הָעִיר הַגְּדוֹלָה	16.	מֶלֶךְ חָדָשׁ
3.	גָּדוֹל הַיּוֹם	10.	אֱלֹהִים בָּאָרֶץ	17.	הַדָּבָר הָרָשָׁע
4.	הַחַי/הַחַיִּים	11.	חֶסֶד גָּדוֹל	18.	הָאִישׁ הַצַּדִּיק
5.	חָכְמָה גְדוֹלָה	12.	יָמִים רַבִּים	19.	אֲבָנִים יְקָרוֹת
6.	אִישׁ חָכָם מְאֹד	13.	הַיָּשָׁר וְהַטּוֹב	20.	עִיר קְטַנָּה
7.	קָדוֹשׁ יְהוָה	14.	אִשָּׁה חֲכָמָה		

B.
1. to another man
2. a living God
3. an evil spirit
4. better than sons and daughters
5. between good and evil
6. YHWH is over many waters
7. the righteous and wicked alike
8. the new heavens and the new earth
9. a numerous people
10. to other gods
11. YHWH is righteous
12. the wicked men
13. YHWH is good and just
14. over mighty lands and over great kingdoms
15. a heavy force and a strong hand
16. the good are very good and the bad are very bad

You Should Know

1. The inflection of adjectives.
2. The attributive, predicative and substantive uses of adjectives.
3. The comparative.

Take Special Note

1. When you use **BDB**, you will need to be familiar
    with the traditional names for verbal patterns.
    Be sure you have learned these correspondences:

    G = **Qal**   HtD = **Hitpa`el**
    D = **Pi`el**          Dp = **Pu`al**
    H = **Hiph`il**        Hp = **Hoph`al**
    N = **Niph`al**

2. **G active participles** are easy to recognize
    because they "ride in on the coattail (קֹטֵל)."
    <u>Know</u> this vowel pattern. Familiarize yourself
    thoroughly with the forms given in the synop-
    sis of the G active participle on p. 47 of
    your <u>Grammar</u>.

Review the Lesson

1. If you learned the endings of the nouns in
    Lesson III, you already know the inflectional
    endings of the participle, with one exception.
    In the fs the ending is ordinarily ת -, not
    ה -. Review the forms given in VII.2, pp.
    46-47.

2. Because the participle is a verbal adjective,
    it has properties of both the verb and the
    adjective.
    a. verbal properties:
        i.   suggests continuous occurrence
        ii. tense (present, past, imminent future)
             must be inferred from context
    b. adjectival properties:

Attributive	Predicative
אִישׁ עֹמֵד	אִישׁ עֹמֵד
"a standing man"	"a man is standing"
הָאִשָּׁה הָעֹמֶ֫דֶת	הָאִשָּׁה עֹמֶ֫דֶת
"the standing woman"	"the woman is standing"

Substantive
אֹהֵב
"one who loves" = "lover"

Compare this chart with the one for adjectives in **Lesson 5** of your <u>Handbook</u>. Notice the similarities.

Check Your Exercises

A.

1.	ms,	עשׂה	11.	fs,	קרא	21.	ms,	ראה
2.	mp,	אמר	12.	ms,	סבב	22.	fs,	ילד
3.	mp,	עלה	13.	fs,	בכה	23.	mp,	בנה
4.	ms,	שׁמע	14.	fs,	יצא	24.	mp,	ירד
5.	ms,	בוא	15.	ms,	ידע	25.	fs,	שׁמע
6.	fs,	עמד	16.	ms,	צום	26.	mp,	בוא
7.	fs,	שׂים	17.	mp,	נתן	27.	mp,	עבר
8.	fs,	ידע	18.	fs,	קום	28.	ms,	שׁוב
9.	fs,	אכל	19.	fp,	הלך	29.	fp,	בוא
10.	mp,	מצא	20.	mp,	עשׂה	30.	ms,	גלה

B.

1. הָעָם הַיֹּשֵׁב בָּאָרֶץ

2. הַבָּא

3. יֹשְׁבִים בָּאָרֶץ

4. יְהוָה עֹבֵר

5. אֱלֹהִים יֹדֵעַ

6. הָאֲנָשִׁים אֹמְרִים לַיהוָה

7. הַיֹּרְדִים אֶל־הַיָּם

8. הָעָם הַשֹּׁאֲלִים

9. פָּרוֹת אֲחֵרוֹת עֹלוֹת

10. לֵב שֹׁמֵעַ

11. וַעֲתַלְיָה מֹלֶכֶת עַל־הָאָרֶץ

12. עַם־רַב הֹלְכִים מֵהַדֶּרֶךְ

13. רָעָה יֹצֵאת מִגּוֹי אֶל־גּוֹי

14. קוֹל קֹרֵא בַּמִּדְבָּר

15. אֹזֶן שֹׁמַעַת וְעַיִן רֹאָה

You Should Know

1. The forms of the G Active Participle.
2. The uses of the G Active Participle.

Take Special Note

1. **Word Order.** Hebrew sentences have a typical word order. This lesson introduces you to the order VERB-DIRECT OBJECT, which may be reversed to emphasize the object: DIRECT OBJECT!-VERB. If an indirect object is present, the typical order is VERB-INDIRECT OBJECT-DIRECT OBJECT. More will be said about word order later.

2. **The use of הִנֵּה.** Your <u>Grammar</u> notes the difficulties posed by this particle for translation (VIII.5.b, p. 56). The examples given on p. 57 should be studied carefully.

Review the Lesson

1. The **independent personal pronouns** are used as the subject of a sentence, often to call attention to that subject. You must commit these forms to memory (VIII.1, p. 52).

2. The **particle אֵת\-אֶת** marks the definite direct object of a verb (VIII.2-3, pp. 53-54). An object is definite if it is a proper name, if it has a pronominal suffix, or if it has the definite article. The definite object marker
   a. is followed immediately by the direct object,
   b. is not translated, and
   c. will take a pronoun as a suffix.
   Since אֵת\-אֶת can also be the preposition "with," you must be alert to the context to translate correctly. Most often it will be the sign of the definite direct object.

3. **Prepositions**, like the direct object marker, can take pronouns in the form of suffixes, or pronominal endings (VIII.4, pp. 54-56). Focus on the suffixes themselves, "types A, B, and C."

	A	B	C
3ms	– וֹ	– ,מוֹהוּ	– יו
3fs	– ,ָה	– ,מוֹהָ	– יהָ
2ms	– ,ְךָ\ ־ָ, כָה	– ,מוֹךָ	– יךָ
2fs	– ,ֵךְ	– ,מוֹךְ	– יִךְ
1cs	– ִי	– ,מוֹנִי	– ַי
3mp	– ,ָם\ ־,ֶהֶם	– ,הֶם	– ,יהֶם
3fp	– ,ָן	– ,הֶן\ ־,ֵהֶנָּה	– ,הֶן
2mp	– ,כֶם	– ,כֶם	– ,יכֶם
2fp	– ,כֶן	– ,כֶן	(– ,יכֶן)
1cp	– ,נוּ	– ,מוֹנוּ	– ,ינוּ

a. Note the differences and similarities between the types of prepositions and their respective pronominal suffixes, distinguishing especially between אֵת as the direct object marker and אֶת as the preposition "with."

b. The particle הִנֵּה may also take pronominal suffixes. Generally speaking, such a construction denotes presence, immediacy, or the like (VIII.5, pp. 56-57).

Check Your Exercises

A.

1. אָנֹכִי עִמְּךָ
2. נָבִיא הוּא
3. כָּכֶם כָּהֶם
4. כָּמוֹנִי כָּמוֹךָ
5. אָנֹכִי זֹבֵחַ לַיהוָה
6. אָנֹכִי נֹתֵן לָהֶם
7. חַיִּים הֵמָּה
8. אָנֹכִי עֹשֶׂה דָּבָר חָדָשׁ
9. אַחִים אֲנַחְנוּ
10. אָנֹכִי בָּא
11. אֲנַחְנוּ אֹכְלִים
12. חָזָק מִמֶּנּוּ
13. כִּי אִישׁ חָכָם אַתָּה
14. בֵּינְךָ וּבֵינִי
15. הַאֵם הִיא
16. הִיא בָּאָה
17. כָּבֵד מִמֶּנִּי הַדָּבָר
18. הוּא בָּא אֵלַי
19. רַע עָלֵינוּ
20. הִנְנִי/הִנֶּנִּי

B.
1. he is a prophet
2. the thing is too difficult for you
3. I am a prophet as you are
4. you are righteous, O YHWH
5. I am with you
6. Rebekah loved Jacob
7. I am God and not a man
8. you are more righteous than I
9. I was not a prophet, and I was not a son of a prophet
10. I am about to send to you Elijah the prophet
11. he was standing beside them under the tree
12. none like him arose after him
13. we are brothers
14. you are a human and not God
15. God is in heaven, but you are on earth
16. from everlasting to everlasting you are God
17. we are passing from Bethlehem
18. you are wiser than Daniel
19. for you are a holy people for YHWH
20. for God is with us
21. I am sending you to them
22. Abraham was going with them
23. Judah loved David, for he was going out and coming in before them
24. the righteous with the wicked
25. the waters under heaven to one place
26. the days are about to come
27. YHWH loves justice
28. we are about to come into the land
29. you and Pharaoh alike
30. the fire and the wood

You Should Know
1. The forms and use of the independent personal pronoun.
2. The forms and use of the definite object marker.
3. The forms and use of the prepositions with pronominal suffixes.
4. The forms and use of the particle הִנֵּה.

Take Special Note

1. **Demonstratives.** <u>Learn</u> the demonstratives listed on p. 60 (IX.1) in your <u>Grammar</u>. In addition, learn the uses of the demonstratives discussed there and at other places in the chapter.

2. Notice that when demonstratives are used as pronouns and as attributive adjectives they conform to the pattern you already know for adjectives.

Attributive	Predicative
הַשַּׁעַר הַזֶּה	זֶה הַשַּׁעַר
"this gate"	"this is the gate"

3. **Relative Clauses.** Study carefully the various translations of the relative pronoun אֲשֶׁר (as well as שְׁ and זֶה) on pp. 61-63 (IX.2) in your <u>Grammar</u>. Keep in mind that אֲשֶׁר tells you that the two phrases which it joins are in <u>some</u> sort of relationship to each other. Thus it is translated by any number of words in English which demonstrate that relationship. Context must be the guide to choose the appropriate English equivalent.

Review the Lesson

1. This lesson introduces you to many **particles**. For the sake of quick reference, here are the new particles and their names. Consult your <u>Grammar</u> if any of these particles and their uses are unfamiliar you (IX.1-5, pp. 60-67).

אֵלֶּה , זֹאת , זֶה	Near Demonstratives ("this," "these")
הֵנָּה , הֵם , הִיא , הוּא	Far Demonstratives ("that," "those")

Lesson 9

אֲשֶׁר (also שֶׁ/שְׁ, זֶה/זוּ/זֹה)	Relative Particle ("which," etc.)
יֵשׁ/יֶשׁ־	Particle of Existence ("there is," etc.)
אֵין (אַיִן)	Particle of Absence ("there is not," etc.)
הֲ	Interrogative Particle (= ?)
מִי	Personal Interrogative ("who?"/"whom"; "whoever")
מַה־ (מֶה/מָה)	Impersonal Interrogative ("what?")
אַיֵּה	Interrogative Adverb ("where?")

Note: contrast the forms of the interrogative particle (הֲ) with the definite article (הַ·) so that you will not confuse them.

2. Notice the way the prepositions בְּ, כְּ, and לְ are combined with the particle מַה־ (IX.5, p. 66).

בַּמֶּה־ = "how?"
כַּמֶּה־ = "how many?" "how much?"
לַמֶּה־ = "why?"

3. Note the idiom מִי־יִתֵּן, "if only," "would that" (IX.5, pp. 65-66).

Check Your Exercises

A.
1. אֶת־הַתּוֹרָה הַזֹּאת אֲשֶׁר אַתָּה שֹׁמֵר
2. מִי חָכָם
3. מִי הָאִשָּׁה
4. הַנֹּתֵן לְךָ אֶת־הַתּוֹרָה

5. ‏הֵם הָאֲנָשִׁים הַיֹּרְדִים אֶל־מִצְרָיִם‏
6. ‏אַחֲרֵי הַדְּבָרִים הָאֵלֶּה‏
7. ‏זֶה הַדָּבָר אֲשֶׁר יְהוָה אָמֵר‏
8. ‏זֹאת הָעִיר הַגְּדוֹלָה‏
9. ‏מִי הָאֲנָשִׁים הָרְשָׁעִים הָאֵלֶּה‏
10. ‏(אֵין הוּא שָׁם or אֵינֶנּוּ שָׁם)‏
11. ‏יֵשׁ בְּרִית בֵּינִי וּבֵינְךָ‏
12. ‏מִי־זֶה הַמֶּלֶךְ‏
13. ‏אֵלֶּה הַשֵּׁמוֹת‏
14. ‏אֵין לָנוּ כֶסֶף‏
15. ‏הֶעָרִים הַגְּדוֹלוֹת הָהֵנָּה‏

B.
1. This is a good man.
2. Is this not David?
3. Who indeed is coming from Edom?
4. What is this thing that you are doing for the people?
5. this great nation
6. from the wilderness and this Lebanon as far as the great river
7. There is nothing new under the sun.
8. Is this Naomi?
9. I am not making this covenant with you alone.
10. There is a God who judges on the earth.
11. These are (the) wicked ones.
12. Concerning these I weep; my eye, my eye runs with water.
13. the Canaanites who were dwelling in that mountain
14. he and the men who were with him
15. the land on which you are lying
16. in this way which I am going
17. Is your father still living? Do you have a brother?
18. YHWH is in this place.

19. The thing which you are doing is not good.
20. Whose daughter are you?
21. O YHWH, who is like you?
22. No one was in the land.
23. There will be neither king nor prince.
24. I am about to send a messenger before you.
25. a great darkness was falling over it

You Should Know

1. The forms and uses of the demonstratives.
2. The forms and various options for translating the relative particles.
3. The common combinations of אֲשֶׁר and prepositions.
4. The forms and uses of the particles of existence and absence.
5. The ways in which a question can be put.
6. The idiom מִי־יִתֵּן and the use of the prepositions בְּ, כְּ, and לְ with the particle מַה־.

Did You Get It?

Translate the following. Cover the right hand column and expose the answers one at a time to check yourself.

1.	אֵלָיו	1.	to him
2.	הִנָּךְ	2.	you (fs) are, it is you
3.	לָהֶם	3.	to them (mp)
4.	בָּנוּ	4.	in/among/with us
5.	מֵהֶן	5.	from them (fp)
6.	כָּמֹוהוּ	6.	like him
7.	אֵינֶנּוּ	7.	he is not
8.	אִתִּי	8.	with me
9.	אֹתִי	9.	me (definite object)
10.	הֵנָּה	10.	they (fp)/those
11.	אַתֶּם	11.	you (mp pronoun)
12.	אֶתְכֶם	12.	you (mp definite object)
13.	עֲלֵיהֶן	13.	upon them (fp)
14.	עִמָּהּ	14.	with her

LESSON 10

Take Special Note

1. **Construct Nouns.** The forms and use of nouns in construct is a crucial lesson. For the purposes of translation it is especially important to be able to determine the absolute form of the noun in construct. Study carefully the construct-noun "Decalogue" (X.2.a-k, pp. 71-74; see below) and the summary provided on p. 74 in your <u>Grammar</u>.

2. **Unpredictable Construct Forms.** Be sure to memorize the unpredictable construct forms listed on pp. 74-75.

Review the Lesson

1. **Definite and indefinite expressions of genitival relationship** (X.1, pp. 70-71).

indef.-indef.	def.-def.	indef.-def.
דְּבַר אִישׁ	דְּבַר הַמַּלְכָּה	דְּבַר לָאִשָּׁה
"<u>a</u> word of <u>a</u> man"	"<u>the</u> word of <u>the</u> queen"	"<u>a</u> word of <u>the</u> woman"

2. **Construct nouns** are often recognizable by predictable changes in form due to the shift of the accent to the governing noun. The following "Decalogue" summarizes these changes (X.2, pp. 71-75).
   - i.   accent shifts forward (except segolates)
   - ii. mp (יִם) and dual (יִם) endings become יֵ :

     מָיִם --> מֵי

   - iii. fs הָ becomes תַ :

     שִׂמְחָה --> שִׂמְחַת

   - iv.   ָ in a final closed syllable becomes ְַ :

     מַלְאָךְ --> מַלְאַךְ

   - v.   ָ or ֵ in an open syllable reduces to ְ :

     שֵׁמוֹת --> שְׁמוֹת

   - vi. final הֶ becomes הֵ :

     מַעֲשֶׂה --> מַעֲשֵׂה

37

vii.   original **aw** contracts to **ô**:

מוֹת <-- מָוְת

viii.   original **ay** contracts to **ê**:

בֵּית <-- בַּ֫יְת

ix.   segolate plurals revert to their *qaṭl, *qiṭl, or *quṭl base:

מַלְכֵי <-- מְלָכִים

x.   qāṭēl becomes qĕṭal:

זְקַן <-- זָקֵן

3. **Two special uses of the construct chain** (X.4, pp. 75-76).

   a. explicative absolute ("wood of gopher" = "gopher wood")

   b. superlative ("song of songs" = "best song"); note that the superlative can also be expressed by making an adjective definite ("<u>the</u> good" = "best")

4. כֹּל (X.5, p. 76).

   a. forms:

     i.   independent = כֹּל

     ii. with **maqqēp̄** = ־כָּל

    iii. with suffix = ־כֻּל

   b. translation:

     i.   with a definite noun = "all" or "the whole"

     ii. with indefinite noun = "each, every, any"

Check Your Exercises

A.

1.	מָקוֹם	11.	אָבִי	21.	שָׂרֵי
2.	יָם/יָ֫ם	12.	אֲחִי	22.	עֲדַת
3.	שְׂדֵה	13.	תּוֹךְ	23.	יֵין
4.	בָּתֵּי	14.	שֵׁמוֹת	24.	מַעֲשֵׂה
5.	אַנְשֵׁי	15.	נַפְשׁוֹת	25.	עֲפַר
6.	אֲרָצוֹת	16.	פְּנֵי	26.	מְלֶ֫אכֶת

38

Lesson 10

7.	יָד	17.	רָאשֵׁי	27.	צִדְקַת
8.	עֲבָדֵי	18.	חָרְבוֹת	28.	בָּנוֹת
9.	עַמֵּי	19.	כְּלֵי	29.	נְבִיאֵי
10.	חָכְמַת	20.	תּוֹרַת	30.	סִפְרֵי

B.

1.	אַחִים	11.	צְדָקוֹת	21.	חֲדָשִׁים
2.	דְּבָרִים	12.	אִשָּׁה	22.	אֹהָלִים
3.	נָשִׁים	13.	עֲבָדִים	23.	הָרִים
4.	מִלְחָמָה	14.	מָוֶת	24.	שָׁנִים
5.	עָרִים	15.	יָמִים	25.	שָׁמַיִם
6.	אָח	16.	יַמִּים	26.	פֶּה
7.	בָּנִים	17.	מַיִם	27.	אֲנָשִׁים
8.	דְּרָכִים	18.	עֵצִים	28.	רָאשִׁים
9.	כְּנָפַיִם	19.	כֵּלִים	29.	יָרֵךְ
10.	דָּמִים	20.	אֲרָחוֹת	30.	קֳדָשִׁים

C.
1. best servant/lowest slave
2. the holiest place
3. work of human hands
4. after the death of Moses the servant of YHWH
5. my holy mountain
6. the inhabitants of Jerusalem
7. fruit tree
8. Moses the man of God
9. a servant of my lord
10. the land of Egypt is before you
11. there are among them men of valor
12. the warfare was fierce against the Philistines all the days of Saul
13. for the entire gate of my people knows that you are a woman of worth
14. for the work of the tent of meeting and for all its service and for the holy garments
15. I am the God of Abraham.
16. all the elders of the land of Egypt
17. these are the names of the Israelites

Lesson 10

18. the daughters of the men of the city were going out
19. the soles of the feet of the priests who were carrying the ark of YHWH the Lord of all the earth
20. O YHWH of hosts, the God of Israel, who is enthroned on the cherubim, you (indeed) are God, you alone, to all the the kingdoms of the earth. You made the heavens and the earth.

You Should Know

1. The uses and forms of nouns in the construct.
2. The unpredictable construct forms on pp. 74-75.
3. The forms and normal translations of כֹּל.

Did You Get It?

Translate the following. Check your answers by referring to the examples cited in Lesson X in your Grammar.

1. בְּבֵית אָבִינוּ

2. מִזְמֹר לְדָוִד

3. בֶּן לְיִשַׁי

4. בֶּן־יִשַׁי

5. יְפֵה־תֹאַר וִיפֵה מַרְאֶה

6. שִׁיר הַשִּׁירִים

40

LESSON 11

Take Special Note

Pronominal Suffixes on Nouns. Notice that
singular nouns take the same suffixal forms as
those which are attached to בְּ and לְ (Type A in the
chart in **Lesson 8** of your Handbook) and plural
nouns take the same forms as those found with אֶל־
and עַל־ (Type C in the chart in **Lesson 8**). <u>These
suffixes are something you already know!</u>

Review the Lesson
1. **Pronominal Suffixes on Nouns** (XI.1, pp. 79-80).
    a. ms noun: attach suffix directly to the
        noun (Type A suffixes)
    b. mp noun: attach suffix directly to the
        noun after removing יִם ending (Type C
        suffixes)
    c. fs noun: attach suffix to the ending ת_
        (Type A suffixes)
    d. fp noun: attach suffix to the ending וֹת
        (Type C suffixes)

2. **Forms of Nouns before Suffixes** (XI.2, pp.
    80-86).
    a. For many nouns, add pronominal suffixes the
        same way you added endings in Lesson III:
        i.   reduce propretonic ָ or ֵ in an open
              syllable, or
        ii.   reduce pretonic ָ in an open syllable.
        iii. If reduction causes two vocal šĕwā´'s
              to come together, use the rule of šĕwā´
              on p. 73 in your Grammar [X.2.k]:
              *צְדָקָתוֹ <-- צִדְקָתוֹ
              *אֲדָמָתוֹ. <-- אַדְמָתוֹ
    b. Geminate nouns show their gemination:
        עַם. <-- עַמּוֹ
    c. Segolates revert to their original **qiṭl**,
        qaṭl, quṭl bases:
        מֶלֶךְ. <-- מַלְכּוֹ
    d. Diphthongs contract:
        מָוֶת <-- מוֹתוֹ
    e. Review the III-י and ו types given in
        X.2.e, pp. 84-86 and the other irregular
        forms in X.2.f-g, p. 86.

41

Check Your Exercises

A.

1.	אַפֹּה	11.	אִשְׁתוֹ	21.	רוּחֲכֶם
2.	זַרְעֲךָ	12.	נָשָׁיו	22.	עָרֶיךָ
3.	מַחֲנֵהוּ	13.	בִּתִּי	23.	שְׁמִי
4.	בִּגְדֶיהָ	14.	עַמִּי	24.	מַלְכֵּנוּ
5.	מַטֵּהוּ	15.	אָבִינוּ	25.	אָחִיךָ
6.	מַטְּךָ	16.	יָדָיו	26.	אַחֶיךָ
7.	עֻזָּה	17.	שָׂדֵהוּ	27.	אֲנָשָׁיו /
8.	עָנָן כָּבֵד	18.	מַעֲשֵׂינוּ	28.	פְּרִיהֶם/פִּרְיָם
9.	שָׂדֶה	19.	פִּרְיִי	29.	בִּנְךָ
10.	עָנָן יְהֹוָה	20.	פִּיהוּ\פִּיו	30.	בֵּיתוֹ

B.
1. (The) breath of life was in his nose.
2. your beautiful (glorious) garments
3. sowing seed
4. your seed after you
5. the holy garments
6. Your cloud is standing over them.
7. the ivory houses
8. the breath of our nose
9. Our father is old.
10. the God of our fathers
11. another spirit
12. a great ivory throne
13. a tent of meeting
14. a spirit of wisdom
15. a mighty tower
16. their mothers who bore them
17. like the ivory tower
18. the smell of his garments
19. all the men of his house
20. all the days of my life

C.
1. Who knows the strength of your anger?

42

Lesson 11

2. seed to the one who sows and bread to the one who eats
3. Your nose is like the tower of Lebanon.
4. from your mouth and from the mouth of your children and from the mouth of your children's children
5. Your loyalty is like the morning cloud.
6. There is none like you among the gods, O my Lord, nor are there deeds like yours!
7. Indeed, your loyalty is better than life!
8. to the wilderness where he was camping (at) the mountain of God
9. How great is your loyalty upon me!
10. This is the camp of God!
11. There is no one to pitch my tent again!
12. The name of YHWH is a mighty tower.
13. This is the word of YHWH to Zerubbabel: "Not by force, not by strength, but rather, by my spirit."
14. My spirit is standing in your midst.
15. I am YHWH who made everything, who stretched the heavens by myself.
16. a life for ("for the price of") a life, an eye for an eye, a tooth for a tooth, a hand for a hand, a foot for a foot
17. I am putting my words in your mouth as a fire.
18. in the year of the king's death
19. Look! The ark of the covenant! The Lord of all the earth is passing before you! (**Note:** since "lord" is in the construct, it should not be translated "the ark of the covenant of the lord," as most translations do. Here the ark appears to be equivalent to the divine presence.)
20. all the servants of Pharaoh, the elders of his household and all the elders of the land of Egypt

You Should Know

1. The pronominal suffixes which are placed on singular and plural nouns, both masculine and feminine.
2. The forms which nouns take when pronominal suffixes are added to them.

LESSON 12

Take Special Note

1. **The Verb System.** The Hebrew verb system is simple and flexible. The key to mastering it is not rote memorization, but understanding the basic principles by which verb forms are generated. You should quickly become acclimated to building and dissecting these forms by concentrating on recognizing and manipulating the three basic parts of each verbal form:
   a. afformatives and preformatives (forms occurring after and before the root);
   b. the three letters of the root;
   c. the characteristic pointing.
   Learning to identify each of these three elements quickly and confidently will save hours of time in reading.

2. **The G Perfect.** Mastery of the G **binyān** in the perfect is <u>essential</u> to mastering the other **binyānîm.** If you have command of the G Perfect, you will recognize the forms of the other **binyānîm** as variations on the basic themes presented here in G. A tip for identifying the G perfect: spot the afformatives of the perfect; look at the vowel under the first (ק) consonant--in all but the 2mp and 2fp, the vowel is ָ. See ָ in the first syllable, think G perfect. Remember, G = **Qal** in BDB.

3. **Word Order.** In its fullest form, the normal word order in a Hebrew sentence is TIME FRAME-VERB-SUBJECT-INDIRECT OBJECT-DIRECT OBJECT. Be alert for a departure from this order, as it generally highlights the "misplaced" part of the sentence. Study carefully section XII.4.b, "Disrupted Word Order" (pp. 94-95 in your Grammar).

Review the Lesson

1. **Afformatives of the perfect** (XII.1, p. 90).

44

3ms	none	(<u>he</u> did)	3cp	‑וּ	(<u>they</u> did)
3fs	‑ָ ה	(<u>she</u> did)			
2ms	‑תָּ	(<u>you</u> did)	2mp	‑תֶּם	(<u>you</u> did)
2fs	‑תְּ	(<u>you</u> did)	2fp	‑תֶּן	(<u>you</u> did)
1cs	‑תִּי	(<u>I</u> did)	1cp	‑נוּ	(<u>we</u> did)

If the final radical of the stem is the same as the consonant of the afformative, it assimilates (XII.2, p. 92): קָטֹנּוּ = נוּ + קָטֹן.

III‑נ verbs also assimilate with afformatives starting with ת: נָתַתָּ = תָ + נָתַן.

2. **Three types of G‑perfect verbs** (XII.2, pp. 91‑92).

   a. **qāṭal:** active‑transitive (שָׁמַר).

   b. **qāṭēl:** stative‑intransitve (כָּבֵד).

   c. **qāṭōl:** stative‑intransitve (קָטֹן).

3. In **translating the the G perfect**, these are your options (XII.3, pp. 92‑93).

   a. completed action (simple past or present perfect):

      עָמַדְתָּ "you stood" or "you have stood"

   b. present state of the subject:

      צָדְקָה "she is righteous"

   c. subject's perspective: יָדַעְתִּי "I know"

   d. instantaneous action: אָמַר "he says"

   e. imminent event ("prophetic perfect"):

      נָתַתִּי "I will put"

4. **Negating the Perfect:** use לֹא before the verb.

Check Your Exercises

A.

1.	זָכְרָה	8.	מָשְׁחוּ	15.	כָּבְדָה
2.	שָׁמַרְתְּ	9.	כָּתַבְתִּי	16.	זְכַרְתֶּם
3.	זָבַרְנוּ	10.	לָקְחוּ	17.	מָלְכוּ
4.	נָתַנּוּ	11.	שְׁמַרְתָּ	18.	חָזְקָה
5.	כָּרַתָּ	12.	זָקַנְתִּי	19.	הָלַכְתִּי
6.	כָּתַבְנוּ	13.	כָּרַתִּי	20.	נָתַתִּי
7.	לָקַחְתִּי	14.	נָתְנוּ		

45

B.
1. "I have loved you," says YHWH.
2. That is the bread which YHWH gave to you.
3. They ate unleavened bread in the midst of their brothers.
4. Indeed, you said, "We have made a covenant with death."
5. I listened to your voice, to everything which you said to me.
6. Is this your little brother of whom you spoke to me?
7. He remembers his covenant forever.
8. Now I know that you are one who fears God. (**Note:** <u>Grammar</u> lacks אַתָּה at end of sentence.)
9. Jerusalem remembers the days of her affliction.
10. I give you a wise heart.
11. He did not eat food all day and all night.
12. He heard that they had annointed him as king in place of his father.
13. Then Manoah knew that he was the messenger of YHWH.
14. At that moment, fire descended from heaven.
15. Is your father, the old man of whom you spoke, well? Is he still alive?
16. God rules over (the) nations; God sits upon his holy throne.
17. I am old; I do not know the day of my death.
18. These are the names of the Israelites who came to Egypt with Jacob.
19. because the work was heavy on this people
20. to the place where he stood before YHWH
21. You love evil more than good.
22. On that day, YHWH made a covenant with Abraham, saying, "To your descendants I have given this land from the river of Egypt to the great river, the river Euphrates."

You Should Know

1. The afformatives of the perfect.
2. The types and meanings of the G-perfect verbs.
3. Normal word order and disrupted word order.
4. The negation of finite verbs.
5. The directive הָ - (XII.6, p. 96).
6. The elements which may interrupt a construct chain (XII.7, p. 97).

LESSON 13

Take Special Note

Much of this lesson are essentially variations
on the basic forms learned in the previous chapter. If necessary, review the afformatives of the
perfect (chart in XII.1, p. 90) and the inflection
of the G perfect (chart in XII.2, p. 91) before
proceeding. Notice that with very few execptions
(principally the II-ʼ/ֹו verbs) your tip-off for
the G perfect, the ָ under the first consonant, is
still present.

Review the Lesson

1. **G Perfect of Verbs with "Weak" Radicals in the
   Root** (XIII.1-6, pp.100-104).
   a. The following chart illustrates the forms
      in which changes occur. If you are
      uncertain of the reason for any change
      shown, refer to your <u>Grammar</u>, pp. 100-102,
      for assistance. Can you identify the
      person, gender, and number of each of
      these forms?

I-Guttural	II-Guttural	III-ה,ח,ע	III-א
עָמַד	בָּחַר	שָׁמַע	מָצָא
	בָּחֲרָה		מָצָאתָ
		שָׁמַעַת	מָצָאת
			מָצָאתִי
	בָּחֲרוּ		
עֲמַדְתֶּם			מְצָאתֶם
עֲמַדְתֶּן			מְצָאתֶן
			מָצָאנוּ
[קְטַל־]	[קְטַל־]	[קָטַלְתְּ]	[קָטַל־]
			[קְטַל־]

   b. The changes in the following forms require
      more sustained attention. Review the forms
      below. If you are stumped by any of them,

47

Lesson 13

refer to your <u>Grammar</u>, pp. 102-104.

[usual]	III-ה	III-ו/י	
[קָטַל]	גָּלָה	קָם	מֵת
[קָטְלָה]	גָּלְתָה	קָֽמָה	מֵֽתָה
[קָטַֽלְתָּ]	גָּלִֽיתָ	קַֽמְתָּ	מַֽתָּה
[קָטַֽלְתְּ]	גָּלִית	קַֽמְתְּ	מַת
[קָטַֽלְתִּי]	גָּלִֽיתִי	קַֽמְתִּי	מַֽתִּי
[קָטְלוּ]	גָּלוּ	קָֽמוּ	מֵֽתוּ
[קְטַלְתֶּם]	גְּלִיתֶם	קַמְתֶּם	מַתֶּם
[קְטַלְתֶּן]	גְּלִיתֶן	קַמְתֶּן	מַתֶּן
[קָטַֽלְנוּ]	גָּלִֽינוּ	קַֽמְנוּ	מַֽתְנוּ

2. **Stative Participles** (XIII.7, pp. 104-105).
   a. Forms--most are identical to those of the adjective, which you learned in Lesson VI (see pp. 39-40 in your <u>Grammar</u>); note, however, the inflection of the participle of מוּת, (XIII.7.b, p. 105).
   b. Translate the stative participle so as to convey the sense of an on-going situation.

3. **Uses of היה** (XIII.8, pp. 105-106).
   a. Statement of past fact or existence of someone or something in the past.
   b. When preceded by the negative particle לֹא, the absence of someone or something in the past.
   c. Possession in the past indicated by the idiom הָיָה ל-.
   d. May mean "become," "happen," etc.

Check Your Exercises

A.
1. חָזְקָה	6. הָיְתָה	11. חֲזַקְתֶּם
2. בָּאָה	7. הָיִֽיתָ	12. גָּֽרוּ
3. בָּאתָ	8. גָּרִי	13. הָיִֽיתְ
4. בָּאִי	9. בָּאָה	14. הָיָה
5. גַּֽרְתִּי	10. בּוֹשָׁה	15. חָטָֽאתִי

48

Lesson 13

16.	מֶחוּ	25.	עֲלֵיתֶם	34.	שָׁבָה
17.	מָחְנוּ	26.	עָשִׂינוּ	35.	שָׁבְתָה
18.	הָיוּ	27.	קָמוּ	36.	רָאִיתִי
19.	בֹּשׁוּ	28.	רָאוּ	37.	שַׁבְתֶּם
20.	מֶחִי	29.	מֵתָה	38.	מָצָאתִי
21.	חָטָאוּ	30.	חָטָאנוּ	39.	שַׁבְתִּי
22.	חָזַקְתָּ	31.	בָּבְִינוּ	40.	עָלְתָה
23.	חֱיִיתֶם	32.	שָׁאֲלוּ		
24.	חֲטָאתֶם	33.	חָיְתָה		

B.
1. הַלַּיְלָה--demonstrative use of the article (see V.7.b, p. 35).
2. Notice the ms ptc. cs. of the III-ה verb, בנה.
4. Disrupted word order--conjunctive ו attached to a noun preceding the verb (see XII.4.b, pp. 94-95).
5. Use of היה (see XIII.8, pp. 104-105).
6. Notice the additional marker of the feminine in the III-ה verb (see XIII.5.b.ii, p. 102).
7. Independent personal pronoun with finite verb calls attention to the subject (see VIII.1.b, pp. 52-53).
8. On מַה־זֶּה, see IX.5.f, p. 66; on the particle of absence, see IX.4, p. 64.
9. On the interrogative ה, see IX.5.b, pp. 64-65.
10. Review the uses of היה, XIII.8, pp. 105-106.
11. Note the accent on סָרָה; contrast this form with that in 8. above (see XIII.6.b.iii, p. 104).
12. Is שָׁם perf. or ptc.? Note the word order to decide (VII.3.b.ii, p. 49, and XII.4.a. ii, p. 94).
14. On the particle of existence, see IX.3, pp. 63-64.
15. Note the form of the III-ה verb, בָּבְִינוּ.
17. Notice the attention drawn to the subject of the second clause by the use of the personal pronoun with the finite verb (see 7 above).

18. Note the vocative and the lack of the article in poetry.
19. Use of היה (see 10 above).
20. See 7 above.
21. On negation of a finite verb, see XII.5, p. 96.
22. הִנֵּה הַמֶּלֶךְ--"here is the king!" (review the uses of הִנֵּה, VIII.5, pp. 56-57).
24. On the interrogative ה, see 9 above; on the particle of absence, see 8 above.
26. עָלְתָה and בָּנָה--see 6. above.
27. עָלְיתֶם--III-ה root.
28. וַאֲנִי--"Now as for me . . .": disrupted word order (see 4 above); אֹתָם--an Isaiah-scroll from Qumran reads אַתֶּם (which reading might you prefer, and why?).

You Should Know

1. The G perfect of I-, II-, and III-guttural verbs.
2. The G perfect of II-ʾ/ו verbs.
3. The forms and uses of the G stative participle.
4. The uses of היה.

Did You Get It?

1. For extra drill on the basic forms of the G perfect, rewrite Exercise 12.A.

2. For extra drill on the forms in this chapter, rewrite the perfects in Exercise 13.A according to groups of person, number, gender (i.e., all the 3fs together, all the 2ms, etc.). Compare and contrast the members of each group.

LESSON 14

Take Special Note

D Perfect. The afformatives of the D perfect
are the same as those of the G perfect. In the
D perfect, however, the middle radical of the root
is doubled (D=doubling), indicated when possible
by a **dāḡēš**. The tip-off vowel under the first
radical is . . See afformatives of the perfect and
., think D perfect. Remember, D = **Pi'el** in BDB.

Review the Lesson

1. **The forms of the D perfect** (XIV.1,3-6, pp. 111,
   113-115).
   a. The following chart illustrates the forms
      of the D perfect, using the 3ms and 2ms as
      representative. Refer to your <u>Grammar</u> if
      any of these forms give you difficulty.

	usual form קִטֵּל קִטַּלְתָּ		
ר,א-II	**ע,ח,ה-II**	**א-III**	**ה-III**
בֵּרֵךְ	מִהַר	מִלֵּא	גִּלָּה
בֵּרַכְתָּ	מִהַרְתָּ	מִלֵּאתָ	גִּלִּיתָ

   b. You have already learned that some conson-
      ants may lose the **dāḡēš forte** when
      followed by **šěwā´** (V.6, p. 35). This holds
      true for the middle radical in the D
      perfect and participle.

2. **D Participle** (XIV.7, p. 115).
   a. See מְ (as in מְקַטֵּל), think D participle;
      confirm by spotting the _ under the first
      radical and the doubling of the second.
   b. Inflected as G participles are (VII.2,
      pp. 46-47).

3. **Translating D verbs** (XIV.2, pp. 111-113).
   a. factitive: קִדֵּשׁ "he makes holy/consecrates"
   b. causative: לִמַּדְתִּי "I cause to learn/teach"

51

Lesson 14

c. denominative: דִּבְּרָה "she speaks"
d. iterative: כָּתַבְנוּ "we <u>keep</u> writing"
e. declarative: צִדְּקוּ "they declare righteous"

Check Your Exercises

A.
1. בֵּרַכְתִּי--compensatory lengthening of ָ since
   ר may not be doubled (XIV.3, pp. 113-114).
2. מְבָרֲכֶיךָ--D particple; see מְ, think D participle;
   notice also compensatory lengthening before ר
   (see 1 above).
4. בֵּרַךְ--see 1 above.
5. צִוָּה--3ms D perfect of III-ה verb. What would
   the 3fs be? (See XIV.5, pp. 114-115.)
6. Contrast the 1cp G perfect verb with the 1cp
   D perfect verb in this line. What are the
   tip-offs in each case? (See **Take Special
   Note** to Lessons 13 and 14 in <u>Handbook</u>.)
7. מְשָׁרֵת--what verb form is this? Why is there
   a ָ beneath the שׁ? (See 2 above.)
8. מֵחוּ--see XIII.6.b.v, p. 104.
   הַמְבַקְשִׁים--note the loss of the **dāḡēš forte** in
   the מ and ק (see V.6, p. 35); notice also that
   the participle in attributive position here
   takes an object in combination with which it
   makes up a relative clause modifying הָאֲנָשִׁים:
   "all the men who sought your life."
10. צִוִּיתָ--see XIV.5, pp. 114-115.
13. עָשׂוּ--see XIII.5, pp. 102-103.
14. הֲלֹא--notice the pointing of this ה. What
    should you think of immediately? (See IX.5.b,
    pp. 64-65.)
15. רָעָחוּ--see XI.1.b.i, p. 80.
16. הָאַתָּה--see 14 above.
17. הִלַּלְנוּ--1cp D perfect (see XIV.1.b, p. 111).
18. כָּמֹנוּ--see VIII.4.c, p. 55.
21. בַּלֵּילוֹת--note the collapse of the dipthong in
    לַיְלָה when the accent moves to the plural end-

52

ing וֹח (see III.3.b.i, p. 18);

שֶׁאֲהֵבָה--3fs G perfect from אהב plus שֶׁ (see IX.2.b, p. 62).

23. אֱלֹהִים--"O God, . . ."

24. עֲוֹן--ms noun in the construct (note propretonic reduction of ָ; see X.1-2, pp. 70-75);
כְּפִיתָ-- see XIV.5, pp. 114-115.

27. עַל--"concerning."

28. הַמְבַכֶּה--see מְ, think D participle (see XIV.7.c, pp. 115-116, esp. the root גלה); for the pointing of the ה attached to the participle, see IX.5.b.ii, p. 65.

29. מְצַוֶּה--see 28 above.

32. עוֹד--עוֹדֶנּוּ plus a suffix: "he was still."

33. עוֹדֶנָּה--see 32 above, only this time 3fs.

38. מְבַקְשָׁיו--mp D ptc. with pronominal suffix. How do you know that the ptc. is plural? (See XI.1.b.ii, p. 79).

39. חָפְרַע--(and other personal names in this verse) see **Glossary**, p. 304;
אֹיְבָיו--singular or plural? (see 38 above and אֹיְבוֹ in the third line below);
מְבַקְשֵׁי--mp D ptc. cs.

You Should Know

1. The forms of the D perfect and D participle.
2. How to translate verbs in the D **binyān**.

Did You Get It?

Write the following forms in Hebrew. Check your answers by the paradigms on pp. 111-116 of your <u>Grammar</u>.

1.	D perf. 3ms דבר	6.	D perf. 2fp גלה
2.	D perf. 2fs בקש	7.	D perf. 1cs שבר
3.	D ptc. mp שרח	8.	D perf. 3fs מכר
4.	D perf. 3ms גלה	9.	D perf. 1cp מאן
5.	D ptc. fs שלח	10.	D perf. 2ms מלא

Take Special Note

H Perfect. The afformatives of this **binyān** are the same as those of the G and D perfects. But the H perfect is tipped off by a prefixed הַ and the ‘ in the second syllable (of third person forms). Remember H = **Hiph'il** in BDB.

There is very little new material in this lesson; in particular, sections XV.3-10, pp. 122-126, mostly involve applying principles you have already learned. Whenever an H-perfect form containing a "weak" radical causes you difficulty, return to review the form of the G perfect with the same radical in the same position (see XIII.1-6, pp. 100-104). Oftentimes the very same principles will apply.

Review the Lesson

1. **The forms of the H perfect** (XV.1,3-10, pp. 120,122-126).

   a. The following chart illustrates the forms of the H perfect, using the 3ms and 2ms as representative.

	usual form הִקְטִיל הִקְטַלְתָּ		
I-guttural	III-ה,ח,ע	III-א	III-ה
הֶעֱמִיד הֶעֱמַדְתָּ	הִשְׁמִיעַ הִשְׁמַעְתָּ	הִמְצִיא הִמְצֵאתָ	הִגְלָה/הִגְלָה הִגְלִיתָ/הִגְלִיתָ
I-נ	I-ו	I-י	II-ו/י
הִגִּיד הִגַּדְתָּ	הוֹשִׁיב הוֹשַׁבְתָּ	הֵיטִיב הֵיטַבְתָּ	הֵקִים הֲקִימֹותָ

Notice that no matter what else happens to the H perfect, you will always find the prefixed הַ.

2. **H participle** (XV.11, pp. 126-127).

   a. prefix is typically מַ (contrast D, מְ)

54

Lesson 15

b. The chart below shows the exceptions to the pointing of the prefixed מ. Notice the similarity to the pointing of the prefixed ה in the perfect.

usual form	before I-ו	before I-י	before II-ו/י
מַ-	מוֹ-	מֵי-	מֵ-
מַקְטִיל	מוֹשִׁיב	מֵיטִיב	מֵקִים

3. **Translating the H** (XV.2, pp. 120-122).
   a. causative: הִמְלַכְתָּ "you caused to rule"
   b. factitive: הִגְדִּילוּ "they made high/exalted"
   c. denominative: הֵיטַבְתִּי "I did well"
   d. declarative: הִצְדַּקְתָּ "you declared righteous"

Check Your Exercises

1. Note the first two verb forms in the H perfect from I-נ and I-ו roots.
2. הִכּוּ--3cp H perfect; find that root: כ is all that is left from נכה. Be alert for these I-נ and III-ה combinations.
3. הוֹשִׁיעַ--I-ו: ישׁע.
4. הִגִּיד--become very familiar with the forms of נגד in the H; you will see them often.
9. הֻכָּה--when you remove the afformative and the prefixed ה, you are left with כ: once again I-נ and III-ה, נכה.
11. הִצִּיל--see the נ hiding in the צ?
12. הֲמִתֶּם--see XV.10.ii, p. 126.
13. מֵבִיא--מֵ clues you to H ptc. from a middle weak root.
14. מוֹשִׁיעֶךָ--מוֹ clues you to H ptc. from I-ו root. How are I-ו roots classified in BDB? (See IV.2.c.i-ii, p. 23.)
16. The relative clause beginning with אֲשֶׁר modifies "nations," and must be included with the subject elements of the sentence in your translation.

Lesson 15

17. מַ--הַמַּפִּים is the usual form of the prefix of
    the H ptc. What else is left? (See 2 above.)
19. מֵ--מְקִים clues you to what type of root in the
    H ptc.? (See 13 above.)
20. הֱשִׁיבֵנוּ--on this form, see XV.10.i-ii, p. 126.
21. הֶרְאָה--almost looks like a feminine form,
    doesn't it? See IV.6, pp. 123-124, esp. the
    note after the chart.
22. הֲקִמֹתִי--see XV.10, p. 126.
23. Notice the disrupted word order throughout
    Nathan's address to David.
    הִבֵּיתִי--see 9 above.
25. הַמַּעֲלֶה is easy enough to recognize as an H ptc.
    from עלה, but what about הַמּוֹלִיךְ?!? (See
    XV.8.b, p. 125.)
27. נָחַתָּ = נָחַתָּה.
28. מַגְדִּל--see XV.2.b, p. 121, for translation.

You Should Know

1. The forms of the H perfect and participle.
2. How to translate verbs in the H **binyān**.

Did You Get It?

1. Write the following forms and check your answers
   by the paradigms, pp. 120-127 in your <u>Grammar</u>:
   3ms of קטל, עמד, שמע, גלה, נגד, ישב, יטב, שׁוּב;
   1cs of קטל, שמע, מצא, גלה, נגד, ישב, יטב, קוּם.
2. To review the basic forms of G, D, and H perfect,
   write קטל in each **binyān** in groups according to
   person, number, and gender (i.e., 3ms in each,
   2ms in each, etc.).

Take Special Note

You must be able to recognize immediately
both the object suffix attached to the verb and
and the form of the afformative of the perfect
before that suffix (XVI.1-2, pp. 131-134). The
following chart will help you recognize the changes
that take place in the afformatives and the distinction between them and the object suffixes of
the same person, gender, and number.

	Object Suffixes	Endings of the Perfect Before Suffixes	Endings of the Perfect
3ms	הוּ/הוֹ/וֹ֫	--	--
3fs	הָ֫/תָּהּ	תַ	הָ
2ms	ךָ/ךָ֫	תְּ	תָּ
2fs	ֵךְ/ֵ֫ךְ/ךְ	תְּי	תְּ
1cs	נִי/יְ֫	תְּי	תִּי
3cp	ם/ָם (m)/ן/ָן (f)	וּ	וּ
2mp	כֶם	תֶּ(תּ)וּ	תֶּם
2fp	--	תֶּ(תּ)וּ	תֶּן
1cp	נוּ/נוּ֫	נוּ	נוּ

You are already familiar with most of these
suffixes from previous lessons. Pay particular
attention to any which are not immediately
apparent to you. In addition, you must know the
changes to the endings of the perfect before the
suffixes (the middle column in the chart).

Review the Lesson

1. Because the accent usually shifts when a suffix
   is added, changes in the pointing of the verb
   may occur--especially reduction in the propretonic or tonic syllables, changes which you
   have come to expect. Note, also, that if the
   addition of a suffix causes a short vowel to
   stand in an open syllable unaccented, that
   vowel will lengthen (XVI.1.b, p. 131):
   שָׁמְרוּ (lengthen) <-- שָׁמֲרוּ* (reduction) <-- וּ + שָׁמַר.

2. **Unusual Forms** (XVI.2-3, p. 135).
   a. III-ה
      i. 3ms loses final radical:
          רָאָה + הוּ = רָאָהוּ
      ii. 3fs loses double gender marking:
          צִוְּתָה + תָּה = צִוַּתָּה
   b. anomalous ָ or ֵ in second syllable (just
      be alert for this so it does not stump
      you): יָלַדְתִּי + ךָ = יְלִדְתִּיךָ

Check Your Exercises

1. בֵּרַכְךָ--You immediately recognize ךָ as a suffix.
   Remove it, and you are left with בֵּרַכ-. There
   is no ending, so it must be 3ms. What **binyān**
   is בֵּרַךְ? (See XIV.3, pp. 113-114).

2. יְדַעְתִּיךָ--ךָ suffix on יְדַעְתִּי, which could be
   either 1cs or 2fs (XVI.1.d, p. 132, or see
   chart above in **Take Special Note**). Look at
   the context, however--אֲנִי is the subject, so
   the verb must be 1cs.

3. וַיְלִדְתְּנִי--י suffix on יְלָדַתְּ-. Which ending of
   the perfect becomes תְּ before a suffix?

4. וַיִּקָּחֵנִי--י again, on לְקָח-. No ending, must
   be 3ms.

5. אֲכָלָתְהוּ--הוּ with אָכְלָת-. The תְ has lengthed
   to תָ in pause (see **Appendix** C.2, p. 290).
   You can confirm that it must be 3fs by looking at the subject of the sentence--חַיָּה רָעָה.

6. אֲכָלוּם--easy enough. ם plus אָכְלוּ-.

7. יְלִדְתִּיךָ--don't let the anomalous ָ throw you
   (see XVI.3, p. 135). The subject (אֲנִי) tells
   you the verb must be 1cs, not 2fs.

8. שָׂמַנִי--remove the suffix נִי-, and you are left
   with a perfect verb with no ending; it must be
   what person, gender, number? On שָׂם-, see
   XII.6.3, p. 103.

10. וַהֶעֱלִיתָנוּ--נוּ suffix on הֶעֱלִיתָ-, which you recog-
    nize immediately as H perfect of a I-guttural
    root (see XV.3, p. 122). When you remove the

58

prefix ה, you are left with only על for your
root, but the י following clues you to think
of III-ה (see XV.6, p. 123; compare XIII.5,
p. 102). The ending is תֶ (from תֶן), the form
which perfect endings take before suffixes?
(See XVI.1.c.iv-v, p. 132.) The form does not
tell you whether the persons being addressed
are masculine or feminine--you must rely on
the context (as given, there is not enough
context for you to know; read Num. 20:2-4).

11. רָ--מְשַׁלְּחֲךָ] suffix on what verb form? (See XIV.7,
pp. 115-116.)

12. צִוִּיתִים--and שְׁלַחְתִּים] suffix on perfect verbs
ending in תִּי. Only context can show you
whether it is 1cs or 2fs. Look at בִּשְׁמִי before
and דִּבַּרְתִּי after these two verbs. Which person
is present?

13. עָנָוִי--take off the suffix; what are you left
with? What perfect form in all **binyanīm**
loses a weak radical before a suffix? (See
XVI.2.a, p. 135.)

14. הִכּוּם--suffix ם. הִכּוּ is left. You should recognize the וּ ending immediately as 3cp and
the הִ as the prefix of the H perfect. The
dāḡēš forte in the כ tells you a נ has assimilated (XV.7, p. 124): נכה.

15. וִיזַבְּחֻנִי--נִי] suffix (יִ lengthened in pause;
see **Appendix** C.2, p. 290). Ending ה before
a suffix can only be one thing.

16. הִצִּילֻנוּ--when the נוּ] suffix comes off, -הִצִּיל
shows no ending; therefore 3ms. Remove prefix
and characteristic vowel of the H perfect,
and you are left with צל. **Dāḡēš forte** in the
צ tells you what? (See 14 above.)
וְאַבְשָׁלוֹם--Note disrupted word order: "But
Absalom . . ." (see XII.4.b.iv, p. 95).

17. וַתֹּאמֶר צִיּוֹן--"And Zion said, ..."

19. הַשְּׁבֵחִים--Did this one stump you? See XVI.2.c,
p. 41.

21. וְיִיֶן וְשֵׁכָר--disrupted word order again (see
16 above).

59

Lesson 16

23. הוּ--צֵוֹּהוּ suffix. What verb in the perfect loses its final weak radical before a suffix in all **binyanīm**? (See 13 above.)

24. ־ה--אֲהֵבָה and שְׂנֵאָהּ suffixes on perfect verb forms without endings. Did the comparative use of מִן sneak up on you?

25. Notice the use of the independent personal pronoun אָנֹכִי before the 1cs perfect verbs.

27. ־ם--צֵוָּם suffix. Did you pick up on the disrupted word order in the third line?

You Should Know

1. The pronominal suffixes attached to verbs, the changes in the endings of the perfect before suffixes, and the kinds of changes in pointing which occur when suffixes are added.

2. The translation (i.e., the lack thereof) of Redundant Object Suffixes (XVI.4, p. 136).

Did You Get It?

1. For extra drill, practice writing the forms illustrated in XVI.1.f. Cover the column on the left and write out the forms. Uncover the column to check your answers.

2. You can do additional drilling on the perfect with object suffixes by using your descriptions (parsings) of forms in the Exercises. As you are translating the sentences in the Exercises, describe (parse) all the verb forms. Write the parsings down on a separate sheet, then write out the forms to fit the parsing, and check your answers by the originals in the sentences.

LESSON 17

Take Special Note

1. **The Imperfect.** In contrast to the perfect, the
    imperfect is signalled by a preformative.
    <u>Learn the preformatives of the imperfect</u>: י,
    ה, א, נ. The imperfect also has its own set of
    afformatives (see below) which will also help
    you distinguish it from the perfect.

2. **The G Imperfect.** A tip for identifying the
    G imperfect: in the "strong" verb (and many
    "weak" verbs, too) the preformative is pointed
    with ִ , except for the 1cs (א). So whenever
    you see ִ under preformative י, ה, or נ, think
    G imperfect. Familiarize yourself thoroughly
    with the inflections of the G imperfect given
    in the chart in XVII.2.b, p. 141. As you did
    in the case of the perfect, you will find
    learning the imperfect much easier if you have
    mastered the basic forms in G before moving
    to the other **binyānîm.**

Review the Lesson

1. **The preformatives and afformatives of the
    imperfect** (XVII.1, p. 140).

3ms	י‎---	3mp	וּ‎---‎י
3fs	תּ‎---	3fp	תּ‎---‎נָה
2ms	תּ‎---	2mp	וּ‎---‎תּ
2fs	תּ‎---‎י	2fp	תּ‎---‎נָה
1cs	א‎---	1cp	נ‎---

Some tips:
a. Notice that only the 3m forms are marked
    by י preformative.
b. Only the 1c forms are marked by a
    preformative א or נ.
c. In the plurals, m forms are marked by an
    וּ ending and f forms by נָה.
d. 2fs stands out as the only form ending
    with י.

    e. Although the 3fs and 2ms are identical, as are the 3fp and 2fp, you will have no difficulty with them in reading, since context will be your guide.

2. **Two types of G-imperfect verbs** (XVII.2, pp. 140-141).
    a. yiqtōl--most transitive verbs (qātal-type; see XII.2, pp. 90-91)
    b. yiqtal--stative-intransitive verbs (qātēl and qātōl types; see XII.2, pp. 90-91)

3. **Translating the imperfect** (XVII.3-5, pp. 141-144).
    a. future: יִמְלֹךְ "he will reign"
    b. habitual: יֹאמְרוּ "they used to say"
    c. modal: אֶשְׁמַע "I should heed"
    d. interrogative present: לָמָּה תִּשְׁאַל "why do you ask?"
    e. injunction: תִּשְׁמֹרְנָה "you shall keep"
    f. jussive (desire for action--third or second person <u>only</u>): תִּגְאַל "let her/may she redeem"
    g. cohortative (speaker's desire or intention to act--first person <u>only</u>); watch for "volitive ה ָ " attached: נִקְרְבָה "let us draw near"

4. **Negating the imperfect** (XVII.6, p. 144).
    a. usually לֹא
    b. לֹא + second person imperfect = prohibition
    c. אַל + second person imperfect = negative command
    d. אַל negates cohortatives and jussives

Check Your Exercises

1. אָמַר--see XII.3.c, p. 93.
2. יִשְׁבֹּן--י preformative: must be 3m; no וּ ending: cannot be plural; 3ms.
3. תִּמְלֹךְ--could be either 3fs or 2ms; the subject, however is אַתָּה, so it must be 2ms.
4. אֶרְדּוֹף--א preformative: must be 1cs; on "full" writing, see II.3, p. 10.
5. See 2 above.

6. יִזְבְּחוּ--י preformative: must be 3m; ו ending: must be plural; 3mp.
11. יִשְׁמְעוּן--see XVII.1.b.ii, p. 140.
12. תִּשְׁמְרוּ--ו ending: must be plural; with ת preformative, must be 2mp.
13. מֵשִׁיב--see XV.11.b.ii., p. 127.
14. נָה--תִּשְׁמַעְנָה ending: must be fp; could be either 2fp or 3fp; since אָזְנֶיךָ is the sub-ject, 3fp.
16. וְשִׁחַרְתֻּנִי--see XVI.c, pp. 131-132, and XVI.e, pp. 132-133.
17. נ--נִשְׂרֹף preformative: must be 1cp.
21. בִּי--"By me . . ."
23. תִּמְשַׁח--could be either 3fs or 2ms; see Exod. 30:22 for the subject.
24. לֹא תִשְׁמַע--see XVII.6.b, p. 144;
    חוֹלֶם--see VII.2, pp. 46-47.
27. יִשְׁאָלוּן--see 11 above.
31. מִ--יִתֵּן--see IX.5.c, p. 65; on translation of the imperfects in this verse, see XVII.3.c, pp. 142-143.
32. אֶזְכְּרָה--see XVII.5, p. 144.
33. וְאֶכְרְתָה--see 32 above.
34. וְנִכְרְתָה--see 32 above.

You Should Know

1. The preformatives and endings of the imperfect in all persons, genders, and numbers.
2. The types and meanings of G-imperfect verbs.
3. The forms and uses of the jussive and cohor-tative.
4. The negation of the imperfect, jussive, and cohortative.

Did You Get It?

Practice writing the forms of the G imperfect using the roots פקד, שמח, שׂרף. Check your answers by the paradigm given at XVII.2.b, p. 141.

LESSON 18

Take Special Note

The material in this lesson is simply a set
of variations on the forms learned in Lesson XVII.
Review the preformatives and endings of the imperfect (XVII.1, p. 140) and the inflection of the
G imperfect (XVII.2, pp. 140-141) before proceeding.

Although in this lesson you will see a variety
of vowels under the preformative, remember: see ˌ,
think G imperfect. If another vowel is present,
you can account for the deviation by noting a
"weakness" somewhere in the root.

Review the Lesson

1. **G imperfect of verbs with "weak" radicals in
   the root** (XVIII.1-8, pp. 148-153).
   a. The following chart reviews the changes
      which occur in the G imperfect. If you are
      uncertain of the reason for any change
      shown, refer to your <u>Grammar</u>, pp. 148-153,
      for assistance.

usual form	I-guttural	III-א	III-ה	I-נ	I-ו
יִקְטֹל	יַעֲמֹד יֶחֱזַק יֹאכַל	יִמְצָא	יִגְלֶה יִהְיֶה	יִתֵּן	יֵשֵׁב (יֵלֵךְ)

	I-י	II-י/ו	יכל		
	יִיטַב	יָקוּם יָשִׂים יָבוֹא	יוּכַל		

   b. Notice that הָיה (and חָיה) do not behave
      as I-guttural verbs in the imperfect, only
      as III-ה.
   c. Review also the 2fs, 1cs, 3mp, and 3fp
      forms in each of the groups noted above to
      get an overview of the variety of changes
      which may occur.

64

Lesson 18

Check Your Exercises

1. אֵלֵךְ--see XVIII.5.c, p. 151; on its translation, see XVII.3.c, pp. 142-143.
2. אֶהְיֶה--see XVIII.3.Note, p. 150.
3. תַּעַבְדוּן--see XVIII.1.d.i, pp. 148-149, and
   XVII.1.b.ii., p. 140.
5. תֹּאמַר--see XVIII.1.c, p. 148.
6. תִּקַּח--note the **dāḡēš** in the ק: see XVIII.4.d,
   p. 151;
   תַּעֲשֶׂה--עשׂה behaves as a I-guttural at the
   beginning (XVIII.1, pp. 148-149) and as a
   III-ה at the end (XVIII.3, pp. 149-150).
7. תֹּאבַד--is this verb 3fs or 2ms? The subject
   of the sentence is תּוֹרָה, so which must it be?
8. תּוּכַל--see XVIII.8, p. 153;
   יָמוּת--see XVIII.7, pp. 152-153; the subject
   of יָמוּת is a proper name (see **Glossary**, pp.
   303-304).
9. יֵשְׁבוּ--see XVIII.5, p. 151;
   וְקַח--note the **dāḡēš** in the ק (see 6 above);
   וְתֵן--the same form as the preceding, but a
   different first radical (see XVIII.4, p.
   150); did you note the examples of disrupted
   word order in this verse?
10. Notice that כָּל־דִּבְרֵי הַסֵּפֶר and רָעָה both function
    as direct objects of the H ptc. מֵבִיא. The
    first is indefinite, but the second is def-
    inite and thus takes אֵת (see VIII.2, p. 53).
11. יָמוּת--see 8 above and XVII.3.c, pp. 142-143.
    Did the interrogative ה stump you?
12. תֵּצֵא--see XVIII.5, p. 151.
13. אִירָא--see XVIII.5.d, pp. 151-152.
14. יִפְּלוּ--**dāḡēš** in the פ: see XVIII.4, p. 150;
    יָשׁוּב, יָקוּמוּ--see XVIII.7, pp. 152-153.
15. אֶשָּׂא--**dāḡēš** in the שׂ: see 14 above;
    יָבֹא-- see XVIII.7., pp. 152-153.

65

16. וְשָׁאֵל--see XVI.1, pp. 131-134;
    יִשָּׁא--see 15 above;
    מַאֲמִינִם--see XV.11, pp. 126-127 (the plural
    ending is written defectively here).
17. יֵשְׁבוּ--on the form, see XVIII.5, p. 151; on
    translation, see XVII.4, pp. 143-144.
18. אָשִׁים--see XVIII.7, pp. 152-153.
19. יִמְעוּ--where is the **dāḡēš** in the מ? (See V.6,
    p. 35.);
    יֶחֱנוּ--I-guttural and III-ה; see XVIII.1, pp.
    148-149 and XVIII.3, pp. 149- 150).
20. Note the G imperfect 2fs forms here.
21. Note the cohortative ה's (see XVII.5, p. 144).
22. Note especially the 2ms and 1cs forms in this
    verse;
    אִם--try translating, "Even if . . . "

You Should Know

1. The G imperfect of verbs with gutturals and
   "weak" radicals in the root.
2. The G imperfect of יכל.

LESSON 19

Take Special Note

Past Narration (XIX.2, p. 159) is fairly straight-forward and should give you little trouble. Should you pick up another Grammar after reading this one, however, some confusion can occur. Your <u>Grammar</u> describes as a **wyqtl** form what other Grammars call a "**wāw**-conversive" or "**wāw**-consecutive with imperfect." The only real difference is that of terminology which, not incidentally, reflects a different understanding of the historical development which led to the form of the verb used for past narration. (Consult XIX.1, p. 158 in your <u>Grammar</u> for a discussion of this process of historical development.)

Review the Lesson

1. **Past Tense Narration and Other Consecutions** (XIX.2-3, pp. 159-160).
    a. You have already learned about sequences (word order) within the typical Hebrew sentence in Lesson 12. In this lesson, you begin to learn how sequence can carry over from one sentence to the next, affecting the way you translate the verbs in the sequence. Here are the sequences you learn in **Lesson 19**:
      i.   perfect + **wyqtl** = past
      ii. imperfect + וֹ-perfect = imperfect
      iii. participle + וֹ-perfect = future

2. **Wyqtl Forms** (XIX.4, pp. 160-162).

usual form וַיִּקְטֹל			
I-א	I-ו	I-י	II-ו/י
וַיֹּאמֶר or וַיֶּאֱהַב	וַיֵּשֶׁב	וַיִּיטַב	וַיָּקָם וַיָּשֶׂם וַיָּנַח
III-ה	III-ה/I-נ		חיה/היה
וַיִּגֶל וַיַּעַן	וַיֵּט		וַיְחִי

Note: Verbs III-ה are irredeemably irregular. You should get used to spotting them because the form in front of you can't be anything else.

Check Your Exercises

1. ם--מִגְּדוֹלָם וְעַד־קְטַנָּם is the 3mp personal pronoun on the end of these two nouns which function as an appositive to the subject: "They put on sack cloth--from the greatest of them to the least." And of course you noticed the **dāḡēš** in וַיִּגַּע: I-נ.

2. וַיֵּלֶךְ--3ms **wyqtl**; become familiar with seeing הלך acting as a I-ו since this is a common verb in past narration. And what else can וַיִּחַן be but III-ה?

3. וּבֵרַכְתִּיךָ--The ךָ is a 2ms suffix and the תִּ is the 1cs afformative, so the root is ברך. What **binyān** is this verb? ר cannot be doubled, so the ַ under the ב is lengthened from an ָ , your clue for the D perfect.
   וַיֵּט--I-נ/III-ה: נטה. See XIX.4.e, p. 163.

4. הֶחֱזַקְתִּיךָ--similar to בֵרַכְתִּיךָ in 3 above (1cs perfect with 2ms suffix) except for the prefixed ה, which is your clue for the H **binyān**.
   מֵאֲסְתִּיךָ--מאס is the root.

5. וַיִּגַּר--see XIX.4.d, p. 161.

6. וַיִּפְנוּ--3mp **wyqtl** from פנה.
   סֻלְמָה--see XII.6, p.96.

7. וּב--this is resumptive and can be left
    untranslated. Notice the two perfects in
    sequence (וּפָנִיתָ / וְהָלַכְתָּ) which should be
    translated as imperfects (XIX.3, pp. 159-160).
8. וַנִּפֶן / וַנַּעַל--If you missed the נ as a 1cp pre-
    formative did you spot the root and look it up?
    III-ה!
9. וַיִּסְעוּ--3mp **wyqtl** of a I-נ verb.
    וָאֶשָּׂא--Note the dāḡēš in the שׂ: this is a I-נ
    verb. The א at the beginning must therefore
    be the preformative of the imperfect. Which
    person, gender and number is it?
13. אַיֶּכָּה--The כָּה is a 2ms suffix which is attached
    to אַיֵּה, hence, "Where are you?" See IX.5.g,
    p. 67.
14. וַיָּרֶץ--see XIX.4.d, p. 161; look in BDB under
    רוּץ.
15. וַיֵּלְכוּ/וַיַּעֲשׂוּ--One of these is pretending to be
    a I-ו, the other is a I-ה. Which is which and
    how can you tell? See XIX.4.c, p. 161 and
    XIX.4.e, p. 162 for clues.
    בַּחֲצִי הַלַּיְלָה--"in the middle of the night" = "at
    midnight".
    הֻכָּה--The ה at the beginning points you to
    the **binyān**. The dāḡēš in the כ points you
    to the first radical of the root. See XV.7,
    p. 124.
    וַתְּהִי--On the form, see XIX.4.e, p. 162. This
    is an example of impersonal narration: "There
    was a great cry in Egypt. . . "

You Should Know

1. The verb sequences used for past narration and
    other verb sequences.
2. The forms of the **wyqtl**.

Lesson 20

Take Special Note

You can speed your learning of the imperative by performing a simple exercise. Take some paper and write the four 2nd-person imperfect forms (2ms, 2fs, 2fp, and 2mp) on it. Now take a pair of scissors and cut off the preformative (תּ). What you have left is the imperative. The only change that needs to be made is to change the first šĕwā in 2fs and 2mp forms to a ִ (i.e.,

תִּקְטְלוּ--<*--קְטְלוּ <--קְטְלוּ ; תִּקְטְלִי--<*--קְטְלִי <--קְטְלִי). This is done in order to avoid having two vocal šĕwā''s in a row (see V.2.b., p. 32 to review the general rules of šĕwā'). This exercise works for the "weak" verbs too, and it explains, for instance, why verbs I-נ do not have their first radical--it was lost in forming the imperfect (see XVIII.5.a.i, p. 151).

Review the Lesson

1. **Forms of Commands** (XX.1-3, pp. 167-172).

	Cohortative (1st person)	Imperative (2nd person)	Jussive (3rd person)
sg	אֶקְטְלָה	קְטֹל קִטְלִי	יִקְטֹל תִּקְטֹל
pl	נִקְטְלָה	קְטֹל קְטֹלְנָה	יִקְטְלוּ תִּקְטֹלְנָה

Things to Note:
- a. Verbs III-ה do not have cohortative forms with the הָ ending but instead use the imperfect.
- b. Verbs III-ה and II-ו/י are the only ones whose jussive forms normally differ from the imperfect:
  III-ה = יִבֶן ; II-ו/י = יָשֵׂם or יָמֹת.

2. **Negating the Imperative** (XX.5, p. 173).
- a. Use לֹא or אַל with the imperfect (not the imperative)! (review XVII.6, p. 144).

3. **Imperatives as Interjections** (XX.7, p. 173-174).
- a. רְאֵה--Behold! Look here!
- b. לְכָה, הָבָה, קוּם--Come! Come on!

70

Lesson 20

4. נָה and לְ with Imperatives (XX.6 and 8, pp. 173 and 174).
   a. נָה expresses emphasis, urgency, or immediacy.
   b. A redundant לְ + the second person suffix sometimes follows the imperative.
5. **More Sequences** (XX.9. pp. 174-175).
   The Imperative is used in narrative sequences to give special coloring to the whole sequence. Here are the sequences detailed in your <u>Grammar</u> in short-hand form:
   a. imperative + ו-perfect = imperative.
   b. imperative + ו-imperfect (<u>not</u> **wyqtl**) or jussive or cohortative = purpose/result.
   c. jussive + ו-imperative = purpose/result

Check Your Exercises

2. שֵׂא--see XX.3.h, p. 171; the ֵ vowel is characteristic of נשא (note the final א).
3. וְנִבְנֶה / נַעֲשֶׂה--The ה ֶ ending tells you the roots are III-ה, while the נ is the 1cp preformative of the imperfect: these are examples of the III-ה's using imperfect forms for their cohortatives (XX.2.b, p. 168).
4. תֵּדַע--see XVIII.5, p. 151.
   מַכֶּה--The מ prefix is the sign of the H participle, and the dāḡeš in the כ tells you that the root is נכה.
5. קַח--the ל of the root (לקח) has dropped off, just like a I-נ (see XX.3.h.ii, p. 171).
6. מֵבִיא--the initial מ tells you this is a participle, but what kind? Notice the characteristic יִ of the H **binyān**. Also notice the sequence in the second line: an imperative is followed by ו-cohortative (see XX.9.b, p. 175).
7. וֶהְיֵה־שָׁם--Be there! = Stay there!
9. בְּבָרָע--בְּ frequently marks the object of some transitive verbs. Notice that the noun is definite, hence the ָ beneath the preposition (see V.1.b, p. 31).

71

10. וַיִּרָא--see XIX.4.e, p. 163.

שֻׁבוּ--see XX.3.g, p. 170.

נָשׁוּבָה / נֵלְכָה--these are both 1cp cohortatives from I-ו (remember הלך acts like a I-ו) and II-ו/י roots respectively. See the list at XX.2, p. 168.

You Should Know

1. The forms of the G Jussive and G Cohortative.
2. The forms of the G Imperative.
3. The use of the particle נָֽא.
4. The use of imperatives as interjections.
5. The use of the redundant dative with imperatives.
6. The narrative sequences using the imperative.

Did You Get It?

Form the G imperative of the following roots. Check your answers by the charts at XX.3, pp. 168-172.

1.	שכב	6.	נתן
2.	עשׂה	7.	ישׁב
3.	היה	8.	שׂים
4.	הלך	9.	עמד
5.	קום	10.	נסע

Lesson 21

Take Special Note

You should review the first two paragraphs of the discussion of the Perfect with Object Suffixes (XVI.1.a-b, p. 131) to remind yourself of the function of this type of construction and the reasons for the vowel changes which occur when suffixes are added to verb forms.

Review the Lesson

1. **The Imperfect and Imperative with Object Suffixes.** (XXI.1.d, p. 180)

3ms	הֹוּ֫	3mp	ﬦָ
3fs	הָ֫	3fp	ן ָ
2ms	ךָ	2mp	כֶם
2fs	ךָ	2fp	--
1cs	נִ֫י	1cp	נוּ֫

a. If the verb ends in a vowel, the "connecting vowel" (ָ or ֶ) is dropped before the suffix: יִשְׁמְרוּ + ֵהוּ = יִשְׁמְרוּהוּ ; but יִשְׁמֹר + ֵהוּ = יִשְׁמְרֵהוּ

b. When the suffix is added, the thematic vowel of the verb may change: ֹ to ָ, ֵ to ָ, and ַ to ֶ (XXI.1.b, p. 180)

c. An additional נ may occur before the suffix, but there is no change in meaning (XXI.1.e, p. 181).

d. III-ה verbs drop the final ה before the suffix (XXI.1.f, p.181).

2. **G Infinitive Absolute** (XXI.2, p.181).

Usual Form	III-ה	II-ו/י
קָטֹל/קָטוֹל	בָּנֹה/בָּנוֹ	שׂוֹם/קוֹם

3. **Translating the Infinitive Absolute** (XXI.3, pp. 182-183). See your <u>Grammar</u> for examples.

a. as a verbal noun.

73

b.   before the verb--emphasis; after the verb--
     continuance or simultaneous action.
c.   with an imperative--intensifier.
d.   in place of an imperative or finite verb.

Check Your Exercises

1.   וְשָׂחוּ --inf. abs. from a III-ה root. In this
     sentence, the infinitives are used in the
     place of imperatives; see XXI.3.e, p. 183.
2.   הוֹצִיא --see XV.8, p. 124.
3.   חֵט --the root is נטה; the form is jussive. See
     XX.1.a, p. 167.
     תַּעַזְבֶה --the preformative ת tells you this is a
     2ms imperfect; the ָה on the end is the object
     suffix. So also with תִשְׁמְרֶךָ and תִצְרֶךָ.
     אֶהָבֶה --again, the ָה is an object suffix. What
     is the form of the verb? See XX.3.e.ii, p. 170
     and XXI.1.c.ii, p. 179.
4.   תִקְבְּרֵנִי --the נִי is the object suffix.
     וּקְבַרְתַּנִי and וּנְשָׂאתַנִי --both are perfects with
     object suffixes. Translate them as imperfects
     since they are in sequence with תִקְבְּרֵנִי (see
     XIX.3.a, pp. 159-160).
5.   דְּרָשׁוּנִי --if נִי is a suffix, then what is דְּרָשׁוּ?
     See XXI.1.c.i, p. 179.
     גָּלֹה יִגְלֶה --see XXI.3.b, p.182.
6.   יַאֲהָבֵנוּ --3mp imperfect with 1cp suffix. The
     "connecting vowel" is _ rather than _ because
     this word is "in pause", that is, it receives
     the final, heaviest accent at the end of a
     sentence (see **Appendix** C, p. 290).
7.   Note the additional נ before the object suffix
     attached to אֶכְתֹּב (אֶכְתֲּבֶנָּה). Notice the "con-
     verted perfects" in this passage (see XIX.3.a-b,
     pp. 159-160). There is also a perfect without
     a **wāw** which must be rendered in the future
     (see XII.3.e, p. 93).
8.   יַעֲנֵם --the root is ענה. See XXI.1.f, p. 181.

74

9. יְנִחֲלֶנָּה--H imperfect with object suffix. This
    is a case of double accusative, as both the
    suffix and "Israel" are objects of the action
    of the verb.
    יִירָשׁוּהָ/אֶתְּנֶנָּה--both are imperfects with object
    suffixes ("I will give it"/"they will possess
    it"). Notice the additional נ in the first and
    the retention of the original I-י in the second.
    סָעַ/וּפֶנוּ--both are ms imperatives. Notice the
    loss of the final ה in the first one and the
    lack of the **dāḡēš** in the second (from נסע)
    because of the loss of gemination in the **s**-
    consonants when followed by a **šĕwā´** (V.6, p.
    35).
    צִוְּהוּ--D perfect (see ַ under the first radical,
    think D!) with object suffix. On the loss of
    the III-ה of the verb in the 3ms with suffix,
    see XVI.2.a, p. 135.

You Should Know

1. The forms of the object suffixes on imperfects
    and imperatives.
2. The forms and uses of the infinitive absolute.

Did You Get It?

Describe (parse) the following forms:

1.	שְׁלָחֲנִי	6.	אֶבְנֶךָ
2.	יִשְׁמָעֵנִי	7.	בָּחוֹר
3.	תִּלְוֵהוּ	8.	בָּנוֹ
4.	יִשְׁלָחֶהוּ	9.	מוֹת
5.	יִשְׁלָחֻנּוּ	10.	שׂוֹם

Lesson 22

Take Special Note

1. **Synopsis of Verb.** Of particular importance in this chapter is the chart on p. 193, "Synopsis of Verbs in G" (XXII.6). The student should review the forms of the verb, particularly those forms which have been a problem. Remember, G = **Qal** in BDB.

2. **More on Sequences.** So far you have seen how word order functions within a sentence (Chapter XII) and how the order of verb tenses functions within a narrative (narrative sequences--Chapters XIX and XX). In this chapter a new wrinkle is added: temporal clauses. These are simply markers telling you in what relationship to the present you should read that which follows in the narrative. They are variations on "Once upon a time." Be familiar with the introductory clauses in this chapter as they occur frequently.

Review the Lesson

1. **Forms of the G Infinitive Construct** (XXII.1-2, pp. 187-190).

usual form קְטֹל		
III–ה	I–ו	I–נ
בְּנוֹת	שֶׁבֶת	נְפֹל or פַּחַת

	II–ו	II–י
	קוּם	שִׂים

Notice the following:
a. הלך acts like a I–ו: לֶכֶת is the inf. cs.
b. Verbs I–ו behave like segolate nouns; thus the form of the inf. cs. with a suffix is שִׁבְתִּי, "my dwelling".

76

Lesson 22

c. Suffixes attached to the inf. cs. show possession, as they do when attached to nouns; but they do not indicate whether the inf. is subjective or objective, that is, whether the suffix is the subject or the object of the action. Context must be your guide.

2. **Translating the Infinitive Construct** (XXII.3, pp. 190-191). See your <u>Grammar</u> for the full example sentences.
   a. As a subject or object of a sentence: שְׁמֹעַ, "obeying"
   b. With the preposition לְ to express purpose: לָלֶכֶת, "in order to go"
   c. With the preposition לְ as a gerund: לֶאֱכֹל, "by eating"
   d. In temporal clauses (see below).

3. **Negating the Infinitive Construct** (XXII.4, p. 191).
   Use בִּלְתִּי with the preposition לְ before it: לְבִלְתִּי שְׁמֹר, "not keeping"

4. **Temporal Clauses** (XXII.5, pp. 191-192).
   a. past events:
      i. introduced by וַיְהִי.
      ii. introduced by כִּי, כְּמוֹ, or כַּאֲשֶׁר + finite verb.
      iii. introduced by בְּ or כְּ + inf. cs.
   b. future events: introduced by וְהָיָה.

Check Your Exercises

1. Notice the variations in the forms of the G inf. cs. found in these verses: I-ו, II-ו, I-נ, I-guttural, III-guttural, and III-ה.
2. עָשֹׂה אֶעֱשֶׂה--see XXI.3.b, p.182. Notice the sequence in the first two lines: imperfect + ו-perfect (see XIX.3.a, pp. 159-160). On הָיָה + לְ see XIII.8.d, p. 105.

3. לֹא יָכֹל לִבְנוֹת--Notice here the way the inf.
cs. with the preposition לְ works with a
finite verb: "he was not able to build"
עַד תֵּת־יְהוָה--inf. cs. in a temporal clause:
"until (such time as) the Lord gave . . . "

4. אֵיכָה--see IX.4,g, p. 67.
לְבִלְתִּי אֲכָל־מִמֶּנּוּ--inf. cs. negated: "not to eat
from it" (see XXII.4, p. 191).
וָאֹכֵל--see XVIII.1.d.ii-iii, p. 149.

5. מִתִּתִּי/יִתִּתִּי--here the suffixes on the inf. cs.
are subjective (the suffix attached is the
subject of the action): "my giving" (or "I
give" for the sake of smooth translation);
notice, too, that the מִ attached to the
second inf. is comparative.

6. וַיְהִי אַחֲרֵי מוֹת מֹשֶׁה--see XXII.5.i, pp. 191-192.

You Should Know

1. The forms and uses of the G inf. cs.
2. The negation of infinitives.
3. How temporal clauses are introduced and translated.

Did You Get It?

Give the G inf. cs. of the following roots:
1. שׁמר   4. נפח
2. עמד   5. לקח
3. ילד

Lesson 23

Take Special Note

1. A **synopsis of the D binyān** is given in
XXIII.4 (p. 201). Review the forms of the verbs in
D. It may be helpful to compare the synopsis of
the D with that of the G in the previous chapter
(XXII.6, p. 193). Remember, D = **Pi'el** in BDB.

2. It is essential to learn the masculine
absolute forms of the **cardinal numbers** given in
the chart at XXIII.5 (pp. 201-202). The other
forms are recognizable as variations on these
basic forms.

3. **Identification Tips.** Notice the ִ under the
preformative of the D imperfect. See ִ, think D
imperfect. Naturally, the 1cs preformative (אֲ)
will be pointed with a ֲ instead of a ִ because it
is a guttural.

Review the Lesson

1. **Forms of the D imperfect** (XXIII.1, pp. 198-200).

	Usual form יְקַטֵּל	
II-Guttural	III-ה, ח, ע	III-ה
יְמַהֵר/יְמָאֵן	יְשַׁלַּח	יְגַלֶּה

2. **Forms of the D Imperative** (XXIII.2, p. 200).
   a. As with the forms of the G imperative (XX.3,
      pp. 168-172), the forms of the D imperative
      are most easily thought of as D imperfects
      with their preformatives chopped off.

	Imperfect	Imperative
2ms	תְּבַקֵּשׁ	בַּקֵּשׁ
2fs	תְּבַקְשִׁי	בַּקְשִׁי
2mp	תְּבַקְשׁוּ	בַּקְשׁוּ
2fp	תְּבַקֵּשְׁנָה	בַּקֵּשְׁנָה

    b. Note the characteristic doubling of the middle radical (when possible) and the pátaḥ under the first radical (unless compensatory lengthening is taking place).

3. **Forms of the D Infinitive** (XXIII.3, pp. 200-201).
    a. In most verbs, the forms of the D infinitive absolute and construct are identical.
    b. The most common pattern is קַטֵּל.

4. **Numbers**
    a. **Cardinal Numbers** (XXIII.5, pp. 201-204).
        i. אֶחָד, "one".
            α. attributive: follows noun; agrees in gender and definiteness.
            β. substantive: precedes noun in construct state.
        ii. שְׁנַ֫יִם, "two".
            α. substantive: stands before noun in construct or in absolute.
            β. agrees in gender with the noun.
        iii. "three" through "ten".
            α. substantive: stands before noun in construct or in absolute.
            β. "Gender switch" takes place: masculine nouns--feminine numbers; feminine nouns--masculine numbers.
        iv. "eleven" and following.
            α. substantive: stands before the noun.
    b. **Ordinal Numbers** (XXIII.6, pp. 204-205).
        i. Except for "first" (usually רִאשׁוֹן, sometimes אֶחָד), ordinals are formed from corresponding cardinals by the addition of a ִי suffix.
        ii. As attributive adjectives, they follow the noun they modify and agree with it in gender and, usually, definiteness.
        iii. Above "ten," Hebrew uses the cardinals for ordinals.

5. **Distributive** (XXIII.7, pp. 205-206).
    a. expressed by repetition of a substantive:
        שְׁנַ֫יִם שְׁנַ֫יִם = "two by two"
        יוֹם יוֹם = "day by day"
    b. expressed by preposition לְ (here: "every") with a number:

לְשָׁלְשֶׁת יָמִים = "every three days"
c.   אִישׁ may be used to express "each":
      אִישׁ חֲלֹמוֹ = "each his own dream"

Check Your Exercises

Ruth 1:1-16
1. Note the use of the infinitive construct in
    the temporal clause with which v 1 begins.
    The second half of the verse contains another
    infinitive construct, this one with the pre-
    position לְ. There are many other infinitive
    construct's throughout this passage.
2. Verse 3 begins with a G **wyqṭl** of a II-ו root
    (see XIX.4.d, p. 161).
3. The first verb in v 4 is missing a **dāḡēš** in the
    שׁ, since this indication of the assimilation of
    a ן is often lost when a **šĕwā´** follows a sibi-
    lant (see V.6, p. 35).
4. Note the negation of the infinitive in v 13
    (see XXII.4, p. 191).

Exodus 4:14-25
1. Verse 14 contains an example of a D infinitive
    absolute preceding a D imperfect to emphasize
    the certainty or force of the verbal idea (see
    XXI.3.b, p. 182).
2. Verse 20--remember that לקח behaves like a I-ן
    (see XVIII.4.d, p. 151).
3. וַיַּרְכִּבֵם--(v 20) is an H **wyqṭl** with an object
    suffix.
4. The first half of v 21 contains a pair of G
    infinitive constructs, the first with the
    preposition בְ and pronominal suffix and the
    second with the preposition לְ. The second half
    of the verse contains a pair of D imperfects.
5. The second verb in v 23 is a D imperative.

You Should Know

1. The forms of the D imperfect, imperative and
    infinitive.
2. The masculine absolute of the cardinal numbers.
3. How to recognize and translate numbers.
4. The methods used to express the distributive.

Lesson 24

Take Special Note

1. By way of review, the chart **synopsis of verbs in H** (XXIV.4, p. 214) should be compared and contrasted with those of the G (XXII.6, p. 193) and D (XXIII.4, p. 201). Remember, H = **Hiph'il** in BDB.

2. **Identification tip:** See _ under the preformative, think H imperfect. Check yourself with the ְ between the 2nd and 3rd radicals of the root.

Review the Lesson

1. **Forms of the H imperfect** (XXIV.1, pp. 208-212). The following chart uses the 3ms and 3fs to illustrate the forms of the H imperfect.

	usual form		
	יַקְטִיל		
	תַּקְטִיל		

I-guttural		III-ח,ע	III-ה
יַעֲמִיד		יַשְׁלִיחַ	יַגְלֶה
תַּעֲמִיד		תַּשְׁלִיחַ	תַּגְלֶה

I-ו	I-י	I-נ	II-ו/י
יוֹשִׁיב	יֵיטִיב	יַגִּיד	יָקִים
תּוֹשִׁיב	תֵּיטִיב	תַּגִּיד	תָּקִים

	הלך	
	יוֹלִיךְ	
	תּוֹלִיךְ	

2. **H jussive and wyqṭl** (XXIV.2, pp. 212-213). The vowel-shifts from imperfect to jussive (see XVII.4, pp. 143-144) and to **wyqṭl** are shown in the following chart:

	imperfect	jussive	**wyqtl**
a. strong verb	יַשְׁמִיד	יַשְׁמֵד	וַיַּשְׁמֵד
b. I-guttural	יַעֲמִיד	יַעֲמֵד	וַיַּעֲמֵד
c. I-נ	יַגִּיד	יַגֵּד	וַיַּגֵּד
d. I-ו	יוֹלִיד	יוֹלֵד	וַיּוֹלֵד
e. I-י	יֵינִיק	יֵינֵק	וַיֵּינֵק
f. II-ו/י	יָקִים	יָקֵם	וַיָּקֶם
g. III-ה	יַגְלֶה	יֶגֶל	וַיֶּגֶל
h. I-gutt/III-ה	יַעֲלֶה	יַעַל	וַיַּעַל
i. I-נ/III-ה	יַכֶּה	יַךְ	וַיַּךְ

3. **H imperative** (XXIV.3, pp. 213-214). As in the G and D, the imperative in H looks like the imperfect without the preformative, except that it is marked by הַ.

2ms	הַקְטֵל	2fs	הַקְטִילִי
2mp	הַקְטִילוּ	2fp	הַקְטֵלְנָה

4. **G passive participle** (XXIV.5, p. 214).
   a. Formed on the קָטוּל pattern.
   b. Most frequently used as an adjective.
   c. May also be used as a substantive.

Check Your Exercises

Gen. 1:1-31.
1. וַיַּרְא--(v 4) Although this verb has a **pátaḥ** following the preformative, a characteristic of the H imperfect, it is in fact a G **wyqtl** of the III-ה root ראה (see XIX.4.e, p. 163).
2. Notice the H **wyqtl** which begins the second half of v 4.
3. וַיַּעַשׂ--(v 7) The form of this verb could be either G or H **wyqtl** (see XXIV.2.c.i, pp. 212-213). Context, however, dictates that it is G.
4. תַּדְשֵׁא--(v 11): H jussive.
5. Notice the participles in vv 11 and 12--an H participle (מַזְרִיעַ) and G active participle (עֹשֶׂה).

6. וַחוֹצֵא--(v 12): H **wyqtl** of a I-י root.
7. Note the two H infinitive constructs with the preposition לְ in vv 14 and 15: לְהָאִיר, לְהַבְדִּיל.
8. Verse 18 contains two infinitive constructs, the first in G (וְלִמְשֹׁל) and the second in H (וּלֲהַבְדִּיל).
9. וְכִבְשֻׁהָ--(v 28): imperative with object suffix.

You Should Know

1. The forms of the H imperfect, jussive, **wyqtl**, and imperative.
2. The form of the G passive participle.

Did You Get It?

Describe (parse) the following forms. Use the paradigms throughout the chapter to check your answers.

1.	יוֹסִיפוּ	6.	אָשִׂים
2.	תַּעֲמִיד	7.	תוֹשִׁיבִי
3.	תַּגְלֶינָה	8.	הַקְטִילוּ
4.	יַגִּיד	9.	כָּתוּב
5.	יַכּוּ	10.	וַיָּקֶם

84

Lesson 25

Take Special Note

Identification tips: In all the strong verbs, there is a ֹ beneath the preformative in the N **binyān**--this is even true for the perfect, since the N stem has a נ preformative in the perfect. Remember, N = **Niph'al** in BDB.

In the imperfect, notice that while the ֹ under the prefix might tempt you to identify the form as G, the first radical of the root is doubly distin-guished from the G. That first root letter has a ֹ for its vowel and a **dāḡēš** within it (G = יִקְטֹל ; N = יִקָּטֵל).

This tip should help you out in spotting the N imperative. The N imperative has a prefixed ה as in the H **binyān**, but unlike the H it has that tell-tale ֹ rather than a ַ (H = הַקְטֵל ; N = הִקָּטֵל).

Review the Lesson

1. **Forms of the Verb in N** (XXV.1,3-6, pp. 218, 220-224).
   a. **N perfect:**

	usual form נִקְטַל נִקְטְלָה		
I-guttural	I-ו	II-ו/י	I-נ
נֶעֱזַב נֶעֶזְבָה	נוֹלַד נוֹלְדָה	נָכוֹן נָכוֹנָה	נִתַּן נִתְּנָה

   b. **N imperfect:**

	usual form יִקָּטֵל תִּקָּטֵל	
I-guttural	I-ו	II-ו/י
יֵעָזֵב תֵּעָזֵב	יִוָּלֵד תִּוָּלֵד	יִכּוֹן תִּכּוֹן

85

c. **N imperative:**

usual form	I-guttural	I-ו
הִקָּטֵל	הֵעָזֵב	הִוָּלֵד
הִקָּטְלִי	הֵעָזְבִי	הִוָּלְדִי

d. **N participle:**
See the charts provided in your <u>Grammar</u>
(XXV.6, pp. 223-224).

2. **Translating the N binyān** (XXV.2, pp. 218-219).
   a. reflexive: נִמְכְּרָה "she sold herself".
   b. middle: וְנִקְהֲלוּ "they gathered (themselves)".
   c. passive of G: וְיִקָּבֵר "he was buried".
   d. stative: וְנִבְחָר "it is choice/best".
   e. reciprocal: וְדִבַּרְתֶּן "you spoke with one
     another"

Check Your Exercises

   Since there is a high concentration of **infinitive constructs** in 1 Kings 3, this exercise gives
you a great opportunity to review this verb form
(see XXII.3, pp. 190-191). Here are the uses of
the infinitive construct (and corresponding
examples in your passage):
1. **As a subject or object.**
   v 7: "but I am a wee youngster--I don't know
going out or coming in." Identify the forms צֵאת
and וָבֹא .
   v 11: "but you have asked for **discernment.**"
Identify the form הָבִין .
2. **With the preposition לְ to express purpose.**
   v 11: "you have asked for discernment **in
order to hear** justice." Identify the form לִשְׁמֹעַ .
   v 4: "Now the king was accustomed to going to
Gibeon **in order to sacrifice** there." Identify the
form לִזְבֹּחַ .
3. **With the preposition לְ, this time as a gerund.**
   v 14: "But if you walk in my ways **by observ-
ing** my statutes and my commandments." Identify
לִשְׁמֹר .

Lesson 25

    v 1: "and he brought her to the city of David until he finished **building** his house." Identify לִבְנוֹת.

4. **As the verb in a temporal clause** (often with the subject appearing as a suffixed pronoun).

    v 1: Identify the components of the phrase עַד כַּלֹּתוֹ and notice the translation given above.

    v 18: "On the third day **after I gave birth** this woman also gave birth." Identify the form לְלִדְתִּי.

5. Notice also the following example of the **infinitive absolute**, used in this case for emphasis:

    v 26: "Excuse me, my lord, give her the living child and **by no means slay it**." Identify the components of the phrase וְהָמֵת אַל־תְּמִיתֻהוּ.

You Should Know

The forms and use of the verb in the N **binyān**.

Did You Get It?

Describe (parse) the following forms: (You may find the charts in **Appendix** B, pp. 270-289 helpful).

1.	מִזַּבְּחִים	4.	נִבְנְתָה
2.	נִרְאָה	5.	יִמָּנֶה
3.	לְהֵירְנִיק	6.	נִכְמְרוּ

87

Lesson 26

Take Special Note

1. **Identification Tips.** The HtD **binyān** is extremely easy to spot: it is the only **binyān** which has a ת (the infixed ת) in the prefix. The only difficult forms are treated in section 4 of this chapter--the sibilants and the dentals. Go over that section carefully. Remember, HtD = **Hitpa'el** in BDB.

2. **A word on oaths.** What makes this idiom tricky is the fact that a **negative** oath is often introduced by אִם (that is, a particle which has nothing particularly negative about it), while a **positive** oath is often introduced by אִם לֹא (which would appear to be negative). It is helpful to remember that the threat part of the oath has dropped off. Adding an appropriate equivalent (in your mind) as you translate might help the sentence make more sense.

For example, the first sentence on p. 234 of your <u>Grammar</u> might read, "By the life of Pharaoh, (I'll be damned) if you depart from here."

This method has the advantage of not reversing the sense of the passage (by inserting a negative) while still showing what is going on.

Review the Lesson

1. **Forms of the HtD binyān** (XXVI.3-5, pp. 228-230).

	usual form	
	הִתְקַטֵּל	
	תִּתְקַטֵּל	

I-sibilant	I-dental	I-guttural
מִסְתַּתֵּר	מִדַּבֵּר	הִתְרַחַצְתִּי
נִצְטַדֵּק	תִּתַּמָּם	

II-guttural	I-ו
יִתְבָּרֵךְ	הִתְוַדַּע
הִתְבָּרֵךְ	הִתְיַלְּדוּ

88

The forms used in this chart obviously come from many different inflections (perfect, imperfect, etc.). They are taken from the illustrations given in your <u>Grammar</u>. See if you can identify the forms in the chart. Check yourself with your <u>Grammar</u>.

2. **Translating the HtD** (XXVI.2, pp. 227-228).
   a. reflexive:
   הִתְקַדַּשְׁתָּ "you sanctified yourself".
   b. reciprocal:
   הִתְרָאוּ "they looked at one another".
   c. iterative:
   הִתְהַלֵּךְ "he walked back and forth".
   d. denominative:
   הִתְנַבְּאָה "she prophesied".

3. **The št binyān** (XXVI.6, pp. 230-232).
   There is only one verb attested in this **binyān**, חוה "to bow down and worship." This verb is often listed as an HtD form of שׁחה in the lexicons, such as BDB, so you should be alert to this confusion on the part of early lexicographers. See your <u>Grammar</u> for the forms of חוה.

4. **Imprecations and Oaths** (XXVI.7, pp. 232-234).
   a. **Imprecations**
   i. Introduced by כֹּה יַעֲשֶׂה אֱלֹהִים וְכֹה יוֹסִף "thus God will do and add more" (and the like).
   ii. Second part if positive: כִּי (or אִם לֹא).
   iii. Second part if negative: אִם.
   b. **Oaths**
   i. Introduced by חַי יְהוָה "As YHWH lives . . . " (and the like).
   ii. Second part if positive: אִם לֹא/כִּי אִם.
   iii. Second part if negative: כִּי לֹא/אִם.

Check Your Exercises

Review of הִנֵּה. Since the particle הִנֵּה occurs prominently in Ruth, take this opportunity to review the uses of הִנֵּה found at VIII.5, pp. 56-57. Your <u>Grammar</u> notes the difficulties for translation posed by this particle. The examples given on p. 57 should be studied carefully to discern the range of usages for הִנֵּה. Several studies of הִנֵּה have appeared in books dealing with biblical narrative. The following is a selection of these analyses of הִנֵּה (The specific examples from Ruth are taken from Adele Berlin, <u>The Poetics and Interpretation of Biblical Narrative</u> [Sheffield: Almond Press, 1983] pp. 91-95).

1. **In direct discourse** (that is, a quotation), הִנֵּה is used to register attention or surprise. When used this way, a good translation is "Look!"

An example is found at Ruth 1:15--"And she (Naomi) said, 'Look (הִנֵּה), your sister-in-law has returned to her people.'"

2. **In narration,** הִנֵּה is used to introduce a figure into an ongoing scene. This use may be translated "at that point".

An example is the beginning of Ruth 2:4--"At that point (וְהִנֵּה), Boaz came from Bethlehem."

3. **In narration,** הִנֵּה is used to denote a shift in point of view, what is called "free indirect discourse"--the narrator tells what a character sees rather than supplying that information directly. This use is difficult to translate adequately.

An example can be found if you look ahead to Ruth 3:8 (this is where Ruth has gone to lie at Boaz's feet at the advice of her mother-in-law) --"At midnight, the man gave a start and turned over (and he saw--וְהִנֵּה) a woman lying at his feet."

You Should Know

1. The forms and uses of the HtD **binyān.**
2. The št verb חוה.
3. The imprecation and oath formulae.

Did You Get It?

Parse the following verb forms:

1. מִתְאַמֵּץ
2. לְהַגִּיד
3. יָבוֹא
4. יִירָא
5. וַיְצַו

PRACTICAL HELP 3:   VERB IDENTIFICATION

1. At various points throughout the study guide, we have given tips on identifying various verb forms. The purpose of this Practical Help is to gather those tips together in a single place and in a more readily accessible form.

2. **G binyān.**
   a. **Perfect:** See ָ in the first syllable, think G perfect (קָטַל/קָטְלָה).
   b. **Imperfect:** See ִ under an imperfect preformative, think G imperfect (תִּקְטֹל/יִקְטֹל).

3. **D binyān.**
   a. **Perfect:** See ִ under the first radical think D. Second check, a **dāḡēš** (doubling) in the second radical (קִטֵּל/קִטְּלָה).
   b. **Imperfect and Participle:** See ְ under the prefixes of these verbs, think D. (מְקַטֵּל/תְּקַטֵּל)

4. **H binyān.**
   a. **Perfect:** The prefix is הִ. Second check, a יִ between the second and third radicals (הִקְטִיל/הִקְטִילָה).
   b. **Imperfect, Imperative, Infinitive, and Participle:** See ַ under the prefixes of these forms, think H.

5. **N binyān.**
   a. **All Inflections:** See ִ under the preformatives of these verbs, think N. Second check, a **dāḡēš** in the first radical of the root in all but the perfect.

6. HtD **binyān**.
   a. **All Inflections:** Look for some varia-
   tion on הַת-- .חַ, יָ,
   מָח, תְּח.

7. Now perform a simple exercise. Turn to
   Appendix B of your <u>Grammar</u> (it starts on
   p. 270), or make a copy you can mark up.
   Go through the inflections of the strong
   and weak verbs looking for the identification markers. Where they are **present**,
   <u>circle</u> them. Where they are **absent**, <u>high-
   light</u> what appears instead (for instance,
   הוֹשִׁיב for the H 3ms perfect of I-ו/י
   verbs).

8. Try to think of some reason for the departure from the norm, or some handy way of
   remembering it. The trick is not only to
   be systematic, but simple as well. **Don't
   try to memorize more than you have to.**
   You'll only confuse yourself.

Lesson 27

Take Special Note

The **geminate verbs** are difficult to master. When you come across a form that does not respond to any reconstruction of its root that you can think of (such as II-ו/י), try geminate!

Review the Lesson

1. **Forms of the geminate verb in G** (XXVII.1, pp. 237-240).

	A	B
perfect	סָבְבָה/סָבַב	תַּמָּה/תַּם
imperfect	תָּסֹב/יָסֹב	תֵּחַם/יֵחַם
wyqtl	וַתָּסָב/וַיָּסָב	וַתֵּחַם/וַיֵּחַם
imperative	סֹבִּי/סֹב	תַּמִּי/תַּם
inf. cs.	סֹב	תֹּם
participle	סֹבֶבֶת/סֹבֵב	תַּמָּה/תַּם

2. **Forms of the geminate verb in N and H** (XXVII. 2-3, pp. 240-243).

	N binyān	H binyān
perfect	נָסַבָּה/נָסַב	הֵסַבָּה/הֵסֵב
imperfect	תִּסַּב/יִסַּב	תָּסֵב/יָסֵב
imperative	הִסַּבִּי/הִסַּב	הָסֵבִּי/הָסֵב
inf. cs.	הִסֵּב	הָסֵב
participle	נְסַבָּה/נָסָב	מְסִבָּה/מֵסֵב

3. **Geminate roots and other roots** (XXVII.4, pp. 243-244).
    Be alert to the fact that geminate verbs often "trade forms" with other weak verbs, I-נ (e.g., יִסֹּב) and II-ו/י (e.g., יָרוּן) in particular. Again, if a verb looks like one of these kinds of verbs but you can't find it in the lexicon, look under the appropriate geminate root.

Lesson 27

Check Your Exercises

1. אֵחַר--(v 5) the root is אחר, and this is a rare contracted form from אֲאַחַר, that is, a G 1cs imperfect.

2. וַיְהִי־לִי--(v 6) "there is to me" = "I have". (Look ahead to v 18, לְמִי־אַתָּה: "to whom are you?" = "to whom do you belong?").

3. וַיִּצֶר--(v 8) G **wyqtl** 3ms from the geminate root צרר.

4. וְהִכָּהוּ--(v 9) the כ is all that's left of the root (נכה).

5. Notice the מִן-comparatives in v 11.

6. הַצִּילֵנִי--(v 12) the ה prefix tells you this is H imperative, while the **dāḡēš** in the first radical is your clue to the I-נ (the root is נצל) and the נִי at the end is a 1cs object suffix, hence, "deliver me!".

7. עֵדֶר עֵדֶר--(v 17) is a distributive: "herd by herd".

8. בְּמֹצַאֲכֶם--(v 20) while this is an unusual form, the verb here is an G inf. cs. with a 2mp suffix, and the בְּ prefix acts as a temporal particle, "when you meet (him)". בְּהֵאָבְקוֹ (v 26) is a similar kind of construction (with the inf. in the N **binyān**), hence, "when he wrestled (with him)".

9. The כִּי אִם's in vv 27 and 29 can be understood as supplying the force of an oath to their two clauses, even though other aspects of the oath formula are lacking.

You Should Know

The forms and uses of the geminate verb.

Did You Get It?

Parse the following verb forms:

1. יַשְׁכֵּם
2. יְבָרֶךְ
3. הֵמַר

4. וַתִּלְקֹט
5. נָצֹב
6. הוֹחִירָה

94

Lesson 28

Take Special Note

The **Dp** and **Hp binyānîm** are among the easiest to spot. They are fairly rare to begin with, and the peculiar first vowel makes it hard for you to confuse these with any other **binyān**. Study carefully the variations on the **u** vowel which marks the Hp. Remember, Dp = **Pu'al** and Hp = **Hoph'al** in BDB.

Review the Lesson

1. **Forms of the Dp** (XXVIII.1, pp. 246-247).

perfect	קֻטַּל	קֻטְּלָה
imperfect	יְקֻטַּל	תְּקֻטַּל
inf. cs.	(גֻּלּוֹח)	
participle	מְקֻטָּל	מְקֻטָּלָה

Note: a. The Dp is the passive of the D.
b. The Dp is characterized by the doubling of the second radical of the verb (just like the D) and by the presence of the "**u**-class" vowel under the first radical which marks the passive voice.

2. **Forms of the Hp** (XXVIII.2, pp. 247-250).

perfect	הָקְטַל	הָקְטְלָה
imperfect	יָקְטַל	תָּקְטַל
inf. abs.	הָקְטֵל	
participle	מָקְטָל	מָקְטֶלֶת

Note: a. The Hp is the passive of the H. The Hp is often used in impersonal constructions ("It was told . . . ").
b. The prefix vowel in Hp before:
i. a strong radical is ָ , sometimes ֻ ;
ii. a guttural or ר is ָ ;

    iii. a ‏נ‎ is ֫ , unless the ‏נ‎ is assim-
          ilated, in which case it is ֫ ;
    iv. roots ‏ו‎/‏י‎ (and geminates) is ‏ו‎.

3. **The Gp** (XXVIII.3, p. 250).
    Gp verbs are vestiges of what was at one point
    a completely separate **binyān**. They now look
    just like Dp or Hp verbs--the only way you can
    tell is if the corresponding active verb is
    normally G and not D or H and if the parti-
    ciple has no ‏מ‎ prefix.

Check Your Exercises

Note the following phrases in Jonah 1-2:

1. In Jonah 1:4b, identify the verb forms in the
    phrase ‏וְהָאֳנִיָּה חִשְּׁבָה לְהִשָּׁבֵר‎. Translate this
    enigmatic phrase ". . . and the ship was about
    to be broken up."
2. In Jonah 1:5, notice how ‏לְהָקֵל‎ expresses the
    purpose of the action of the first verb.
3. In Jonah 1:11, identify the verb forms in the
    phrase ‏כִּי הַיָּם הוֹלֵךְ וְסֹעֵר‎. ‏הלך‎ carries the
    connotation of continuous action, especially
    as an inf. abs. but also at times as a ptc.,
    as here (see XXI.3.d, p. 183). Translate this
    phrase ". . . for the sea was growing stormier
    and stormier."
4. The infinitive construct used to express purpose
    is at work in 1:13, ‏לְהָשִׁיב‎, and in 2:1, ‏לִבְלֹעַ‎.

You Should Know

1. The forms and uses of the Dp **binyān**.
2. The forms and uses of the Hp **binyān**.
3. The forms and uses of the Gp **binyān**.

Did You Get It?

Parse the following verb forms:

1. ‏נִרְדָּם‎   4. ‏וַהֲטִילֵנִי‎
2. ‏יְסֹבְבֵנִי‎   5. ‏נִגְרַשְׁתִּי‎
3. ‏וְנַפִּילָה‎   6. ‏בְּהִתְעַטֵּף‎

Take Special Note

The verbs in this chapter are extremely irregular, making it hard to give any specific tips in learning to spot them. Be assured, however, that they are not that hard to spot when you come across one in a text--they don't look like anything else!

Review the Chapter

1. **Qōlēl, qōlal and hitqōlēl verbs** (XXIX.1, pp. 253-255).
    a. characterized by a ו after the first radical and reduplication of the third radical.
    b. tend to occur with II-ו/י and geminate verbs.
    c. take on the meaning of the D, Dp, and HtD.
    d. forms of these verbs:

	qōlēl	qōlal	hitqōlēl
perfect	קוֹמֵם	קוֹמַם	הִתְקוֹמֵם
	קוֹמְמָה	קוֹמְמָה	הִתְקוֹמְמָה
imperfect	יְקוֹמֵם	יְקוֹמַם	יִתְקוֹמֵם
	תְּקוֹמֵם	תְּקוֹמַם	תִּתְקוֹמֵם
imperative	קוֹמֵם	--	הִתְקוֹמֵם
	קוֹמְמִי	--	הִתְקוֹמְמִי
inf. cs.	קוֹמֵם	--	הִתְקוֹמֵם
ptc.	מְקוֹמֵם	מְקוֹמָם	מִתְקוֹמֵם
	מְקוֹמְמָה	מְקוֹמְמָה	מִתְקוֹמְמָה

2. **Qilqēl, qolqal, and hitqalqēl verbs** (XXIX.2, p. 255).
    a. characterized by repetition of first and last radicals.
    b. occur most frequently in geminate verbs (some II-ו/י 's).
    c. take on the meanings of the D, Dp, and HtD.
    d. examples are found in your Grammar.

Lesson 29

3. **Minor patterns** (XXIX.3, pp. 255-256).
   a. **Qōṭēl, qōṭal, and hitqōṭēl** verbs: behave like the **qōlēl** type but have three radicals rather than two.
   b. **Qaṭlēl, quṭlal** verbs: retain all three radicals and reduplicate the third, thereby appearing to have four root letters.
   c. **Qĕṭalṭal and qōṭalṭal** verbs: have all three radicals and reduplicate the last two, thereby appearing to have five root letters.

Check Your Exercises

Use Psalm 95 as an opportunity to review the cohortative. Go back to XX.2, p. 168 to review the forms of the cohortative and to XVII.5, p. 144 to review its meanings. Now translate Psalm 95, paying particular attention to the cohortative verbs in this text and their meanings.

You Should Know

1. The forms and uses of the **qōlēl, qōlal**, and **hitqōlēl**.
2. The forms and uses of the **qilqēl, qolqal**, and **hitqalqēl**.
3. The forms and uses of the **qōṭēl, qōṭal**, and **hitqōṭēl**.
4. The forms and uses of the **qaṭlēl** and **quṭlal**.
5. The forms and uses of the **qĕṭalṭal** and **qōṭalṭal**.

Did You Get It?

Parse the following verb forms:

1. וְנִפְלֵאוּתָיו   4. נֹסֵוּנִי
2. אָקוּט   5. מְהַלֵּל
3. זָרֵעַ   6. הַמִּתְהַלְלִים

PRACTICAL HELP 4:   VERB DESCRIPTION

1. By this point, you have been exposed to the whole Hebrew verb system. It might be helpful at this time to present in a chart the various features which you must take account of in describing (parsing) any particular verb form:

	bin-yān	tense/ state	p/g/n	prefix/	suffix	root	mean-ing
perf.	x	x	x/x/x	--	x	x	x
impf.	x	x	x/x/x	--	x	x	x
impv.	x	x	-/x/x	--	x	x	x
inf. abs.	x	x	-/-/-	--	--	x	x
inf. cs.	x	x	-/-/-	x	x	x	x
ptc.	x	x	-/x/x	x	x	x	x

   a. The letters p/g/n in the third column stand for person/gender/number.
   b. Where the "x" appears in the chart, you must take account of that feature, either spotting it or eliminating it, before you having fully accounted for that kind of verb.
   c. Where the "--" appears in the chart, that feature need not be taken account of for that kind of verb.

2. The easiest way to illustrate how this works is to go through a few examples (these examples are taken from previous exercises).
   a. יְבָרֵךְ--the יְ preformative and the compensatory lengthening under the בּ identifies this as a D imperfect. Now look on the line of the chart for the imperfect. This is how it reads:

	bin-yān	tense/ state	p/g/n	prefix/	suffix	root	mean-ing
impf.	x	x	x/x/x	--	x	x	x

   This indicates that the only thing which can be left unaccounted for is a prefix (such as a prefixed preposition).

99

We can see that the verb has no suffix
attached, and so we proceed:

יְבָרֵךְ   D   impf.   3ms   ברך   "to
                                                bless"

Everything has been taken account of which
needs to be.

b.   הוֹתִירָה--the הו looks like the preformative
of H perfect for I-ו/י verbs, so we look
on the line of the chart for the perfect:

	bin-yān	tense/state	p/g/n	prefix/suffix		root	mean-ing
perf.	x	x	x/x/x	--	x	x	x

With the perfect, as with the imperfect,
we needn't concern ourselves with prefixes. Again seeing no suffix, we proceed:

הוֹתִירָה   H   perf.   3fs   יתר   "to
                                                leave"

c.   נִפְלָאוֹתָיו--The נ preformative tells us we're
in the N binyān. In the N, it's often hard
to tell the difference between the perfect
and the participle. In this case, however,
the fp noun ending (וֹת) leaves no doubt
that this is a participle. So we look at
that line of the chart:

	bin-yān	tense/state	p/g/n	prefix/suffix		root	mean-ing
ptc.	x	x	-/x/x	x	x	x	x

In the case of the participle, only the
person of the verb can be taken for
granted. In the form before us, there is
no prefix attached (the נ being a preformative denoting the N rather than a
prefix). There is, however, a suffix, and
we must mention it in our description:

נִפְלָאוֹתָיו   N   ptc   fp   3ms   פלא   "to be
                                               wonderful"

Practical Help 4

d. מְהַלָּל--The מ preformative tells us this is
some sort of D participle, and the "u-
class" vowel beneath the first radical is
the sign of the passive, or Dp **binyān**.
This participle has neither prefix nor
suffix, and so it can be described very
easily:

מְהֻלָּל   Dp   ptc   ms   הלל "to
                                                praise"

e. בְּהִתְעַשֵּׁף--The **binyān** in this case is easy--
HtD. This verb has a prefix attached, the
preposition בְּ. Looking at the chart, we
see that only the ptc. and the inf. cs.
can take a prefix. As this verb lacks the
characteristic מִתְ of the HtD ptc, it must
be the inf. cs. So we look at the line of
the chart for the inf. cs.:

	bin-yān	tense/state	p/g/n	prefix/		suffix	root	mean-ing
inf.cs.	x	x	-/-/-	x	x	x	x

We needn't worry about the person, gender
or number of the verb, and there is no
suffix in this case, so we proceed:

בְּהִתְעַשֵּׁף   HtD   inf cs   prep. בְּ   עטף "to be
                                               faint"

f. וַנְּסּוּ'--This is a difficult form, because
there appear to be too few radicals to
reconstruct a root. The first syllable (נ)
could either be the sign of the N perfect
(in which case the root would be סוּן), or
the sign of the D perfect (in which case
the root is נסה). (It can't be D perfect
from נסן, since no perfect form has ו
between the second and third radicals). We
have two choices; why not look them up?
When we do, we see that the second option
is the correct one, and we recognize the
dāḡēš in the ס as the sign of the D. A
glance at the chart tells us that we
needn't worry about prefixes. We do have a

101

suffix, however (בֵּ׳), and we include that in our description:

וַנְסֻֿ֫וּ׳   D   perf   3cp   1cp suff.   נסה "to test"

3. Only a great deal of practice will make this second nature, but with the help of your chart, you should be able to describe any verb form without leaving anything out.

Lesson 30

Take Special Note

The aim of this chapter is to introduce you to
some of the subtleties of Hebrew prose. This is
one way to get out of the need to translate the
conjunction וְ as "and" every time. Far from being
less "literal," such a handling of the text in
fact reflects an awareness of what the original
hearer or reader would have understood. Just think
of the variety of relationships which are comuni-
cated by our word "and" due to voice inflection,
verb sequences, additional prepositions, and the
like.

Review the Chapter

1. **Hendiadys** (XXX.1, p. 258).
    This construction is the simple juxtaposition
    of nouns by means of the conjunction when ordi-
    narily you would expect a noun and a modifier.
    An example: עִיר וּמִגְדָּל , "a towering city"

2. **Casus Pendus** (XXX.2, p. 258).
    Casus pendus occurs when the narrator wants to
    emphasize the subject. This is done by isolat-
    ing the subject at the beginning of the sen-
    tence and sometimes inserting the conjunction
    between it and the main clause. The conjunc-
    tion is in this case superfluous.
    An example:
    הָאֵל תָּמִים דַּרְכּוֹ , "God's way is perfect"

3. **Circumstantial Clauses** (XXX.3, pp. 258-259).
    These occur in sentences where the second
    phrase describes some aspect of the circum-
    stances accompanying the main idea of the
    sentence. They are introduced by וְ . An
    example:
    נִבְנֶה־לָּנוּ עִיר וּמִגְדָּל וְרֹאשׁוֹ בַשָּׁמַיִם
    "Let us build ourselves a towering city with
    its top in the heavens."
    --(Note that the second phrase, "with its top
    in the heavens" is a description of "a tower-
    ing city.")

4. **Conditional Sentences** (XXX.4, pp. 259-260).
   a. **Real Conditions.** The protasis ("if" clause) of a conditional sentence is normally introduced by אָם, though less frequently by כִּי, הֵן, or אֲשֶׁר. The apodosis ("then" clause) is sometimes, though not always, introduced by ו. An example:

   אִם־תַּעְצְרֵנִי לֹא־אֹכַל בְּלַחְמֶךָ

   "If you detain me, then I will not eat your food.

   b. **Hypothetical Conditions.** If the sentence is describing something which in fact is not the case, then the protasis ("if" clause) is introduced by לוּ or לוּלֵי/לוּלֵא. An example:

   לוּלֵא חֲרַשְׁתֶּם בְּעֶגְלָתִי לֹא מְצָאתֶם חִידָתִי

   "If you had not plowed with my heifer, then you would not have found my riddle."

   c. **Virtual Conditional Sentences.** These are sentences which context tells you must be conditional, but the usual pointers listed above are missing.
   An example: וְעָזַב אֶת־אָבִיו וָמֵת

   "If he leaves his father, then he will die."

Check Your Exercises

As you translate Genesis 42, take special care to be attentive to the various relationships between clauses and sentences expressed by the conjunction ו and note them on a separate sheet.

You Should Know

1. The construction of hendiadys.
2. The construction of casus pendus.
3. The construction of circumstantial clauses.
4. The construction of conditional sentences-- real, hypothetical, and virtual.